EXTRAORDINARY PRAISE
LINDA RICHMAN AN

I'd rather laugh

"A fast-rising star in the world of personal growth....[The] no-nonsense perspective of one of America's most famous Jewish mothers."
—*Newsweek*

"Linda Richman has lived through a lot and learned as she went along. This book is full of no-nonsense Linda-isms. It will enrich your life."
—Rosie O'Donnell (from the Foreword)

"A terrific book! Linda's advice on how to hold a 'pity party' is brilliant and, in itself, worth the cover price. If humor and resilience were a competitive sport, this woman would be a World Champion."
—Harriet Lerner, author of *The Dance of Anger*

"Earthy, funny, and sensible....Yes, there is a real woman behind Mike Myers's 'Coffee Talk' caricature of Linda Richman...and has she got some stories!"
—*Publishers Weekly*

"A self-help book without the trappings....This book is worth reading not just when 'life has other plans for you,' but in everyday situations."
—*Midwest Book Review*

A Featured Alternate of The Literary Guild®, of Doubleday Book Club®, and of Doubleday Large Print®

more...

"Through her own unforgettable stories, Linda Richman teaches us that the human spirit is always capable of laughter, even after great sorrow. She is a healer who speaks to the heart as well as a messenger of hope. It is my wish that everyone who has ever suffered a profound loss will read this wonderful book."
—Deepak Chopra, bestselling author of *How to Know God: The Soul's Journey into the Mystery of Mysteries*

"Linda's experiences understandably could have led her to the depths of despair and a lesser life. However, her gift of seeing the world from a slightly askew and humorous perspective has created an indomitable spirit. Her heartache is real but so is the wisdom and resiliency gleaned from difficult and painful life lessons. As she shares her story with the reader, she shares her gift of healing, inspiration, and discovery of life's meaning."
—Dan Baker, Ph.D., director, Life Enhancement Program, Canyon Ranch

"Easy to read and filled with Linda's life stories....There are pearls of wisdom interspersed with pathos....Linda is earthy and at the same time profound in her struggle to understand her life and impart wisdom to the reader."
—Herbert S. Cohen, Ph.D., author of *Snap Out of It*

"A shot-in-the-arm book about renewal and redemption...vastly entertaining, yet moving and irrevocably life-affirming."
—Yitta Halberstam, coauthor of *Small Miracles*

"Linda Richman proves to us that laughter is truly the best medicine and that it's not your position but your disposition that makes the difference."

—Cherie Carter-Scott, Ph.D., author of *If Life Is a Game, These Are the Rules*

"In this wise and wonderful book, Richman shows us how to triumph over adversity with love and laughter—and a good dental plan."

—Rabbi Wayne Dosick, author of *When Life Hurts*

"A very engaging book. Don't be fooled by the fast river of punchline humor. You'll find genuine comfort and wisdom here, too."

—Martha Whitmore Hickman, author of *Healing after Loss* and *Such Good People*

"A special book by a special person that provides heartfelt and often hilarious examples of that ancient Hasidic wisdom: 'When you're hungry, sing. When you're hurt, laugh.'"

—Allen Klein, author of *The Courage to Laugh*

"By writing I'D RATHER LAUGH, Linda Richman has given all survivors of loss a wonderful gift. Courage, honesty, and humor are at the core of her resilience. With true generosity and humility, she shares those lessons she learned in the depths of despair. Her dynamic example offers hope to all who face the same struggles and gives perspective to all who cope with everyday losses and disappointments."

—Maxine Harris, Ph.D., author of *The Loss That Is Forever*

I'd rather laugh

How to Be Happy Even When Life Has Other Plans for You

Linda Richman

WARNER BOOKS

An AOL Time Warner Company

Copyright © 2001 by Linda Richman
All rights reserved.

Warner Books, Inc., 1271 Avenue of the Americas, New York, NY 10020
Visit our Web site at www.twbookmark.com.

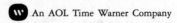 An AOL Time Warner Company

Printed in the United States of America
Originally published in hardcover by Warner Books, Inc.
First Trade Printing: March 2002
10 9 8 7 6 5 4 3 2

The Library of Congress has cataloged the hardcover edition as follows:

Richman, Linda.
 I'd rather laugh : how to be happy even when life has other plans for you / by Linda Richman.
  p. cm.
  ISBN 0-446-52676-2
  1. Laughter. 2. Wit and humor—Psychological aspects. 3. Happiness. I. Title.

BF575.L3 R53 2001
152.4'3—dc21   00-042345
ISBN 0-446-67807-4 (pbk.)

Cover design by Flag
Cover illustration by Geoff Spear
Book design by Giorgetta B. McRee

For Jordan, whose spirit still lives and whose short life had so much meaning. JR, this book is for you.

To my daughter, Robin, the great love of my life. Thank you, my child, for all the joys and all the pleasures you have brought to me. May God keep you safe.

Contents

Foreword   xiii

1. You're Probably Wondering Why I Invited
   You Here   1

2. My Mother, Myself?   7

3. The Incurable Homebody   27

4. Losing Jordan   37

5. The First Laugh Is the Hardest   51

6. How to Throw a Pity Party   59

7. Try It, It Works for Me: Creative Catastrophizing   71

8. Issue? I Hardly Know You!   79

9. A Tale of Two Sammys   95

10. Try It, It Works for Me: Waving the Red Flag   101

11. Travels in the Spirit World   109

12. "Coffee Talk" or Me?   133

Contents

13. More Travels in the Spirit World   143

14. You Talkin' to Me?   153

15. Try It, It Works for Me: The F-Word   161

16. Help Yourself (or Don't)   169

17. Try It, It Works for Me: The Good News   179

18. Jews in Cyberspace   189

19. Try It, It Works for Me: The Wise Fool   199

20. In Search of Your Inner Control Freak   201

Epilogue   217

Acknowledgments   221

Foreword
by Rosie O'Donnell

Here are the things you need to know about Linda Richman. She lied to Dixie Carter, and she abandoned me.

The Dixie Carter story is the easiest, so let's start there.

Wendy Wasserstein had a new play opening on Broadway. I got two tickets and asked Linda to go with me. Opening night, celebs galore—I knew she would love it. She was living with me at the time, one of her many "I'll-come-for-a-week"-and-stays-for-three-months visits. Not that I mind, 'cause I really don't. (The part in the book where she writes that she always leaves after three days . . . pure fabrication.)

So we got dolled up and trotted to the St. James Theater. *An American Daughter*, starring Hal Holbrook. We had great seats, fourth row center. There was an empty seat on the aisle, then me, then Linda.

Enter Dixie Carter. She sits in the empty seat, I give her a kiss hello, ask her if she's nervous for her hubby, Hal, then introduce my friend Linda. Linda reaches over me, grabs Dixie's hand, and never lets go.

"You know what, Dixie Carter?" she said breathlessly. "My daughter, Robin, and her husband, Mike Myers, celebrate your birthday every year!"

Dixie smiled, nodded, and looked confused. I tried to evaporate.

She continued. "Yes, yes, yes, every year on his birthday, May 25th, they get a cake that says 'Happy Birthday, Mike and Dixie Carter!' Can you believe that? Happy birthday to Mike and you, Dixie Carter!"

When the lights went down, I thought I was having a stroke. Nope, turns out it was just divine intervention. The play started.

I whispered angrily to Linda, something along the lines of, *"Are you insane? What's wrong with you? Icannotbelieveyoujustmadeupthatwholefarkaktastory! Iwillnevereverbeseenwithyouagaininmywholelife!"*

She shushed me and told me it was rude to talk during a performance. By intermission she was calm, cool, and collected, swearing the story was true. It wasn't. Two hours later, she fessed up, laughing all the way up Broadway.

"It just flew out of my mouth! I have no idea what made me say it! Isn't that a riot? I knew she and Mike had the same birthday, and before I knew it, I had a cake with their names . . ." By this point, she was too hysterical to talk.

In short, Linda Richman is nuts.

Read this book. See for yourself just how crazy she is. She has no qualms about showing you her psyche, warts and all. She can laugh about it, and I bet you will, too. I know Linda very well. I enjoyed this book, although she chose to omit a few key points. One was that she lied to Dixie Carter; the other is even more horrific. Read on.

She abandoned me.

I met Linda at the premiere of *Exit to Eden*, the worst movie ever made. She came over to me and introduced herself. I felt like I knew her—she was familiar, she was funny, she was friendly. We talked for a few minutes and said our good-byes.

A few years later, I happened to rent a house right near her daughter Robin. Linda was living there (although she will swear she was only there for three days, so as not to wear out her welcome). I was a new and nervous mom, having just adopted my son Parker. Linda and Robin came by to say hi and see the baby. She was very maternal, very New York, and we became fast friends.

She became Grandma to Parker, then Chelsea, and once again to Blake. We did holidays together. I was the child she lost; she was the mom I never had. Bliss. I depended on her and looked to her for advice and guidance, for support and love. She sold her condo on the Upper East Side (she has more money issues than Tammy Faye Bakker) and moved in with me, for *way* more than three days. It worked for me, for her, and for everyone in the free world.

Then one day, she was gone.

Yep. She took a job in Arizona at a health spa. Being a coward, she didn't say good-bye; she just got up and left. In short, she abandoned me.

Now, I'm sure she has her side of this story, but I don't really care to hear it. This is my foreword. You only get my side. Tough. The fact is, she abandoned me, and I was really, *really* mad.

I sulked. I acted like a fourteen-year-old. I rebelled. I was snotty to her, wouldn't return her calls, didn't invite her to things. And to her credit, she never quit. I hung up on her, she hung in there. She would say, "I know you love me, and I love you, and I'll be here when you need me!"

I'd answer her with something catchy like, "Whatever."

Eventually, she wormed her way back into my heart. It's a place where she belongs. She is kind to almost everyone, and she cries at TV commercials. She loves fast food and Barbra Streisand. She's a loving Jewish mother and a compassionate friend.

She has lived through a lot and learned as she went along. This book is full of no-nonsense Linda-isms. It will enrich your life, as she has mine.

Oh, and the part where she says she only reads self-help books? Another lie. She also reads biographies.

You're Probably Wondering Why I Invited You Here

I'm not supposed to be writing this book.

Which means you're not supposed to be reading it, so quick, put it down and go find something else to do. Take a walk, get some fresh air.

Okay, get back here.

I'm not supposed to be writing this or any other book because I'm supposed to be a basket case by now. I'm supposed to be totally defeated and deflated by circumstance and fate. I'm supposed to be a sad situation—mentally, emotionally, psychologically, spiritually, and any other way you can think of. A walking tragedy. The person about whom you say, "There but for the grace of God . . ."

At any rate, I'm not supposed to have anything remotely useful or helpful or worthwhile to share with you. I'm certainly not supposed to be in any position to teach you a thing or two.

And yet, here we are, you and me.

I'm not exactly sure why you're here. I'm not exactly sure why *I'm* here, to be honest with you. Except that through no fault of my own, I have learned quite a lot about life and what it can put you through. Now, I know that we've *all* learned a lot about life, but believe me, some of us have picked up more than others. As I say, it's not because I really wanted to learn so much. There have been a few lessons I could have lived without. But I learned them all the same. And then I learned a few things more.

What did I learn?

I learned that we can withstand a lot of pain and loss and not just survive it but rise above it. I learned that no matter how sad you are today, happiness and laughter and even joy are still distinct possibilities for tomorrow, or if not tomorrow, the day after that. And I learned that you and I have in our power the ability to get all that and more. Everything important is in our control. Everything necessary is ours to decide. It's work. But it's all there, waiting for us to make up our minds.

Okay, I hear you saying, Ms. Big Shot, tell me how.

I can't. It's different for everybody. I don't have your directions. I can't draw your map. Look, I couldn't draw *my* map—it took me a while to find my way. It was a hell of a journey too, a lot of starts and stops and wrong turns and backing up and doing it over. A lot of wondering if I was headed in the right direction. A lot of wondering if there *was* a right direction.

But there was. And there is. And if I could find it, believe me, *you* can find it. I can even help you, if you'll let me.

One night not long ago I actually had dinner with Deepak Chopra.

"Tell me, Deepak," I said, "what's the most important thing you have to teach people?"

"We are the tinkers of our taughts," he said.

"We are the tinkers of our taughts," I repeated. "What the hell is that?"

He said it again.

Even when I finally figured out what he was saying, I knew it wasn't going to work for me. Deepak Chopra is a brilliant man who sells millions and millions of books and has millions and millions of followers. But nobody wants to hear a chunky Jew from Queens saying, "We are the tinkers of our taughts." Life doesn't work that way.

But I also have a message for people. It's fairly simple. I tell them that no matter what horrible thing has happened, life still offers you humor if you want it. I say that regardless of how low you feel today, someday you'll find something that will make you laugh your head off. I guarantee that you'll sing and dance once more. I promise that if you will only make a small effort, you will rediscover happiness.

Sounds like complete and utter bull, right?

It does. I know it. It sounds like bull, and yet people believe me. Sophisticated, intelligent adults, many of them with impressive educations and astronomical net worths, sit in a room and listen. Despite what they know of the world and what it can be like, they take my stories away with them. And if the word of these people can be trusted, sometimes I actually even help.

Why do these people listen to me? Maybe it starts with how I make their acquaintance. In my weekly lecture at Canyon Ranch, the fancy spa in Arizona, the first few minutes are devoted to a video clip showing the brilliant comic actor Mike Myers—who just happens to be my loving and devoted son-in-law—doing one of his most celebrated skits, the Coffee Talk Lady from *Saturday Night Live*—the character who just happens to have been inspired one hundred percent by me.

That breaks the ice. That lets everybody know they're in for a couple of hours of fun and merriment.

Then, once everybody in the room is laughing and giddy and relaxed, I give them a few biographical details from the real Linda Richman. Right between the eyes.

I start by telling them how my father was killed by a truck when I was eight years old. My mother, who had been severely depressed all her life, went into a tailspin with that. The first thing she did was decide not to tell me that my father was dead. Instead, she created a conspiracy of silence within the family. I was informed that my dear, loving dad had just "gone away," never to return home. Imagine the good things that might do to a little girl's psyche. My father's death left my mother totally unable to care properly for me and my older sister. At age nineteen I escaped my lot in life, or so I thought, by getting married, to a lawyer. It started out blissfully—we said we wanted a family soon, and I was pregnant within three months. And then, in short order, my mother was institutionalized and began receiving electroshock treatments, and I discovered that instead of a knight in shining armor, I'd married a gambling addict.

I dealt with all that by escaping into a form of behavioral insanity—I gradually turned into an agoraphobic and stayed inside our apartment for eleven, count 'em, eleven years. I got over that too, but still the bluebird of happiness didn't nest in my bouffant hairdo. My husband's gambling habit finally overtook him, costing us our home, car, furniture, and everything else of value. We divorced, and I would have been literally homeless if not for the kindness of family and friends. And *then* things finally got better, right?

Well, for a while they did. But a year after the divorce my twenty-nine-year-old son was killed in a car accident.

That little tale gets everybody's attention in a hurry, let me tell you. That stops the chuckling. Not that I really want to kill the cheery mood in the room. It just happens. And anyway, most of the people who come to my lectures do so because they are in some pain of their own.

I am an expert in surviving pain with a smile on your face at least some of the time. And that's the main reason people believe me. I'm not coming at them with nine Ph.Ds. I'm not a mystic or a swami. I was put here on this earth to be a teacher, I firmly believe, but one who teaches from the heart. I had to experience things first before I could tell people how to deal with them. I had to know great loss before I could talk about how to go on living after it. It couldn't come to me from a book, and, take it from me, I've tried it that way. I've read every book on spirituality and the soul that I can find. It all helps. But for somebody like me, the useful answers aren't up in the clouds.

People relate to me because I am like them. Whether they're from Nebraska or Queens or Los Angeles, it doesn't matter. They've all suffered. I stand up there as naked as can be and tell them all the terrible stuff that's happened to me and all the crazy, desperate things I've done in response. And then all the things I've done to bring myself back from the abyss and restore the joy.

It's one thing to hear your $150-an-hour (excuse me, fifty minutes) shrink say that if you do this, this, and this, you'll laugh again. It's another, I think, to hear it from me.

But we'll see, right? We have a whole book ahead of us here. Come on, let's get going.

My Mother, Myself?

2

She couldn't have been a bigger influence in my life had she been the greatest mother of all time.

Unfortunately, she wasn't.

Everything since then has been a reaction to her.

How bad was it? You tell me.

All my childhood I wished my mother had died instead of my father.

That's pretty bad, right? I know I should feel horrible confessing that, but I really don't—it's how I honestly felt.

How could I love her? She was homely. Can any little girl love a homely mother? She was slovenly too. Bad teeth. Frayed around the edges. Didn't make an effort.

I used to tell her the wrong week for open house at school, because I didn't want my teachers or my friends and their parents to know what she looked like.

There were no hugs or kisses between us. I hated to touch her. I couldn't even bear to touch her bedclothes, because they had been on her skin.

My mother and my older sister, Judy, had the same birthday, which would have made some kids jealous, but not me. I was actually relieved—if Judy was closer to her, I reasoned, then I must be closer to my father. The fact that I preferred to be closer to my dead parent than my live one says a mouthful, doesn't it?

Oh, sure, there were reasons she was the person she was. But everybody has reasons. Hitler had reasons, I bet. If you want to go through life inflicting misery on yourself, be my guest—it's your right. But once you have a child, you lose the privilege to be as negative and depressing as you want. You've got to do a little better. A child deserves more than your excuses.

She was orphaned before she was ten years old and sent with her sister and two brothers to live in a Catholic orphanage run by nuns. Clearly, the kids should have been in a Jewish institution, but the system did what it did and there you have a little girl already on the road to being screwed up for life. When she got old and sick, my mother would only go to Catholic hospitals. The nuns would take good care of her, she figured. The crucifix hanging over the bed made her feel safe. And when the priest came in the room to see if she wanted a visit or maybe even Holy Communion, well, she was in heaven, no pun intended. Jews of her generation are almost always a little queasy in the presence of priests and nuns, but there she was, as Jewish as can be, at home in the lap of the Catholic church.

Her sister, my Aunt Pat, didn't stay at the orphanage for long. She was adopted by their mother's one surviving sister. My mother never got over that awful rejection, being left behind. But there were four siblings, more than their aunt could have managed. Aunt Pat was the young one, and the pretty one, much more so than my mother. Fair or not, my mother always believed that was why their aunt didn't take her too.

We're all formed by our early experiences, and I think those years really scarred my mother's psyche. I can't even guess what that life must have been like, so it's hard for me to judge. But I can tell you this: Suffering didn't do her personality any wonders. We always want victims to be sympathetic characters. We wish they would be spiritual and full of virtue as a result of all that pain. We want their suffering to make them appreciate whatever good is in their lives. But it doesn't work that way. Suffering doesn't make you a nicer person. Usually it has just the opposite effect.

For example, as a result of her childhood my mother was a terribly jealous person all her life. If somebody did well, Mom always had something snide and insulting to say. Their gain, she believed, was coming right out of her pocket. In fact, as a little girl her sister's good fortune *did* come at her expense. She never got over that. Anytime she saw anybody succeed, she reacted in exactly the same way.

As I said, this is perfectly understandable. Maybe some people have the internal wherewithal to overcome their suffering and remain good and generous and kind. Those are the true heroes—the ones who can suffer and not be warped and destroyed by it.

But we can't all be heroes. My mother failed that test. Lots of people do.

The funny part—and there's nothing funny about this, really, except that it makes me laugh—is that because my mother lives on in me, she even manages to keep her jealousy and pettiness alive.

Her childhood friends, Rose and Sid, later married each other. I say they were friends, although my mother was always finding a reason to be angry with them. They didn't do enough. They didn't call. When they went to Florida, they didn't visit. They were actually very nice people, and

I liked them a lot. To her, though, despite the fact that they were friends she had known all her life, they were always found wanting.

Anyway, recently both Rose and Sid got sick. In fact, he died not long ago, in his nineties. She's still alive at this writing, in her late eighties.

I heard they were ill so I called their daughter and said, "You know what, I want to come and visit your parents."

"Oh," she said, "they'll be thrilled."

"Good," I said, and hung up, full of resolve.

And then I looked in the mirror and said, "I can't go."

I called my sister and said, "Judy, Mother just came back from the dead."

"Oh, really?" Judy said.

"Yes," I replied. Then I told her the whole story, and how the fact that our mother was dead and buried and therefore highly unlikely to know about the visit made no difference. I could just feel her seething with anger when she heard I had gone.

"Rose's children never visited me!" she'd say. "Don't you visit her!"

So I didn't go. Couldn't go. You still need proof of an afterlife? My mother's soul is alive and well and taking up space inside my head. She's always been there, and she'll always be there. She's pure essence now, a life force—a demented, dark, jealous, unhappy life force.

Maybe she wasn't so bad when my father was living. He died when I was eight, so I don't actually recall. I don't remember a single thing about him—every memory I have of Daddy was put in my head by my sister.

He was a cab driver who died while doing a favor for a fare—a young mother with a baby asked him to pull over, run into a store, and get her a bottle of milk. As he was crossing the street, a truck ran him down. This happened while my entire extended family was in the Catskills, at what was called a bungalow colony—a kind of working-class summer resort. One night, with no explanation, the entire family had disappeared and I was left in the care of an aunt whom I hated. The whole time we were together she never said a word to me. Then everybody came back, only they were all crying. Whispering. Staring at me. Clearly, something awful had happened, but what? "Nothing," my mother said when I asked. Then, later, she amended that: "Daddy had to go away." Nothing more. What did I know? I was eight years old. I wished somebody would tell me *something*. Nobody did.

Can you imagine anything sicker? Did my mother really think she was sparing me anything by shutting me out of my own father's death? That's why nobody told me anything, or so I've been informed. They wanted to save me the agony. They didn't think I could bear such a loss. I want to go back there to that exact moment in time and just scream my guts out. I want to make them tell me what happened.

All the sadness and the loss, and the great big lie, form immediately into a terrible black cloud. The cloud hangs over our heads from that moment on. My father is dead, which is tragic enough for a little girl, but as far as I know he just took off and never came back. Clearly, my mother didn't think it through—it was just a stupid decision she made and then got stuck with. But I got stuck with it too. I made up a little story of my own—he had left my mean mother, gone to California, and taken up with a Spanish woman with whom he had five children. Believe it or not, that was actually a consolation to me.

As a child I was in a constant state of anger and sadness about my life and my mother, which seemed totally intertwined and equally depressing. I didn't even have another parent to turn to—she was it. I was completely dependent on her. Do you see why I might have been a bit worried? A little anxious? We had nothing like what you'd call a normal relationship. I have no recollection of a conversation with her—the only words I recall are, "Clean up your room, do your homework," and the like. Granted, she was emotionally sick, and probably had some bad brain chemistry going as well. On top of that, she was a widow with two daughters to raise and not enough money. We had to depend on relatives to kick in so we could live. Better women have been crushed by lesser burdens, I guess. But it was my life too, and I was even more in need than she was. I was a kid.

I built up a lot of rage and resentment toward my mother over the course of my childhood. Naturally, that kind of fury has to come out one way or another. It came out of me when I was around nineteen years old. This is the story of the worst thing I've ever done, and it was a pretty shitty thing, too.

Once again my world was falling apart.

My beloved Aunt Pat, my mother's sister, was the closest thing to a real mother in my own life. I loved her in the way I wished I felt (but did not) about my mother. Aunt Pat was beautiful, with bright red hair, and she was good to me all my life. In fact, she was the great love of my life, and I was the apple of her eye. She was the only person who ever made me feel special—I was smart, she told me, beautiful, clever. Her view of me gave me such joy—once she told me, "Linda, you wheel a shopping cart so well," and I even took pride in that. Any self-confidence I had as a child came from being with her. She *talked* to me. That alone made her unique in my life.

And then she got breast cancer. Figures, right? Once again I'm about to lose somebody I love. She was wasting away. She was in pain. And she knew and I knew that it wasn't going to get any better. This was forty years ago, remember, back when breast cancer meant probable death. Today, thank God, it's a different story. Had it been now, it's likely they would have saved Aunt Pat.

Finally, she died. All the pain that I had been carrying around inside me, like a stone, since my father had died came rushing to the fore. I felt worse than I should have felt. I think now that I really wanted to spread some of that pain around. And I knew exactly where I wanted it to go.

I had to break the news to my mother. She was lying in her bed, depressed, but alive.

"Your sister died," I snarled at her. I tried to make it as painful as possible.

But it wasn't bad enough, evidently. I looked at her. And she looked at me. And I looked at her. And she looked at me. I hated my mother on many different occasions in my life, but never more than at this particular moment.

Slam!

I slugged her! I did! I don't know what exactly came over me, because I was never a violent person up to that moment in my life. And ever since then, forty years later, I remain a pacifist and a coward when it comes to physical violence.

Pow!

I socked her! I knew I would be ashamed later, but boy did it feel good right then and there. It was a lifetime of pent-up anger and rage and hurt and resentment that was coming out of me. I was turning my pain into her pain, at least for a moment or two.

Slap!

I hated to stop! Which I did, of course. She was dazed and confused. I was dazed and exhausted. Was any daughter ever more ridiculous than I was at that second? A hale and healthy young woman beating up her bedridden mother? I was not going to win the B'nai Brith Daughter of the Year award at that rate. I didn't go around bragging about what I had done, to be sure. I told my sister. She wasn't too hard on me. She knew what I was feeling, even if she didn't feel the same way.

And I have to confess that I have never really been consumed by guilt over that shabby little incident. I didn't lose a lot of sleep. I didn't waste too much time agonizing on the shrink's couch. Due to circumstances beyond her control, my mother caused me a lot of pain and suffering. So, due to circumstances beyond my control, I returned the favor. In fact, I caused her about five minutes of pain and suffering, and her life was already doomed to be one of misery and unhappiness. Whereas she caused me many, many years of unhappiness, and, worst of all, she did it to a little girl who was just getting her start in life.

You could say that I'm letting myself off the hook for a despicable act, to which I reply: Hey, if I don't let me off the hook, who will?

Dinnertime was perhaps the most depressing ritual of my childhood. By this point my sister Judy was practically an adult, out with her friends or, later, living nearby with her husband. When my mother wasn't in the hospital, she worked most of the time. So dinner was a meal I normally consumed alone. It consisted of the same thing night after night—a can of Franco-American macaroni, or sometimes ravioli, heated up in a small pot, consumed on a tray in front of the TV. I was still too young to actually cook anything, but heating up I could manage. To this day, I refuse to eat pasta or anything with tomato sauce on it, I don't care which gourmet chef made it.

On the nights when my mother was home, it wasn't any better. Then it would be a table for two—two extremely unhappy females, the younger one barely able to look at the older. There were no long, loving, mother-and-daughter talks over those meals, I promise you.

But just next door to us, a magic ritual was played out night after night. There, the Burkes lived—Pauline and Dave, and their kids, Rhoda and Joel. I can't believe I still recall their names so vividly, considering that I haven't seen them for more than four decades. Lots of nights I'd be at the Burkes's playing when 6 P.M., the hour of magic, rolled around. I'd be told, gently, that it was time for me to scoot on home for my own supper. The door was ever so lightly closed on my heels as I walked out. The whole experience felt like a knife in the heart, but it was thrilling, even glamorous too. I had no idea what dinnertime was like there, but I just knew it was exactly like it was on all those TV shows: the table for four. I can still recall the feeling of being excluded, shut out from something wonderful. Every time, filled with sadness and longing, I skulked back home to my TV tray. Today I know what was taking place there: dinner. But back then it captured my imagination like nothing else.

For years, that picture in my imagination—the table for four—haunted all my daydreams. I wanted that too, at any cost. Which is just about what it came down to. I was in such a hurry to flee my mother that I married too young, before I really knew who I was or what life was about, and I stayed in a bad marriage for thirty years—all thanks to my quest for the mythic table for four. I tried my best, believe me, but I never quite got it. How could I? I had no idea what a happy family life might be like. I didn't know how it was supposed to work when there was Mom and Dad and a couple of kids. I had a husband and two children and a table. But our table was missing something. Not just a chair, either—it was missing a whole leg. It was a very shaky table for four. The marriage didn't work for a number of reasons, none of which I'm going to explain. (I'm saving that one for another book.) But I can say this: Even simply trying to have that table for four nearly killed me, which goes to show how the sweetest dreams can do you the worst damage.

Once I had children of my own, I was determined to avoid all my mother's mistakes and flaws. She never once played with me, so in addition to being my kids' mother, I was their playmate. My childhood was joyless. Theirs, I decided, would be filled with joy. My childhood was gloom and doom. Theirs would be fun and games.

For example, I allowed my son, Jordan, and my daughter, Robin, to draw and write on their bedroom walls. How are you going to encourage artistic expression if you insist that kids express themselves only on some little piece of paper while sitting at a table? That didn't sound very free to me. So if they wanted to use the walls as their canvas it was fine. It was better than fine! It made me happy. Now, this was back in the early sixties, remember, when a woman's house was measured by its cleanliness and order. So people thought I was nuts to let my children scrawl on their bedroom walls, but I didn't care.

They had no curfew once they were teenagers either. They could come in when they were ready. I assumed they wouldn't stay out if they had homework to do or a big day to rest for. So no big scenes with me yelling and pointing at my watch and them sulking and making up excuses for being late.

When I saw and heard my friends disciplining their kids, I would just cringe. To me, they came across like Jack the

Ripper. I hated it. I thought it was so punishing, so destructive to a child's emotional well-being. I let my kids get away with an awful lot. I would even admonish my friends for being so hard on their children. (Of course, they'd tell me to mind my own goddamn business.) I had a good friend whose children were in bed at 7:30 on the dot every night. Meanwhile, at our house it would be midnight and Jordan and Robin would still be wandering around. Sometimes they'd be walking into walls, they were so exhausted, but still they were up.

Or I'd hear my friends hope and pray their precious little ones might grow up to be doctors someday, and I'd be filled with horror at the thought. All that studying and discipline and hard labor? Cutting open cadavers and memorizing chemicals? Who would wish that on their own flesh and blood? I wanted my kids to be artists, or actors, anything creative and liberating and fun.

Now, be honest—how much of a screwball was I? I was intent on sparing my children the kind of miserable existence I had endured as a child. They ended up enduring their own weird childhood. In my eyes, their experience was a walk in the park compared to the dark, depressing, mostly loveless time that my early life had been, true. But I went so far in trying not to be my own crazy mother that I ended up becoming a different crazy mother.

Between the writing on the walls and the no-punishment policy and the lack of curfew or any other structure, they kind of drifted through childhood. The demands were few, the boundaries were almost nonexistent, and that added up to an environment of extremely low expectations. And when you expect little from kids, they take a message from that— nobody cares what I do. If nobody minds when I fail, then nobody will be thrilled when I succeed. If my parents aren't determined that I do well, why should it be such a big deal to me? I had no idea these were the unspoken messages I was sending, but they were. This was the unconscious layer of our relationship, the emotional undertow.

Plus, where I had a crazy, depressed mother who worked all day, they had a crazy, depressed mother who was totally housebound. Knowing that Mom isn't going to show up for parent-teacher conference day is kind of liberating, but it takes some of the joy out of any triumphs you might have enjoyed at school. Knowing that there's some weird thing in Mom's head that has kept her from leaving the house—for the last eleven years—must have killed some of the joy of childhood, wouldn't you say? (Even now, when I think of it—eleven years! It took less time to win World War II! It took less time to build the atom bomb! It took NASA less time to put a man on the moon than it took for me to go from my living room to my driveway!)

As a result, my children had no goals propped up in front of them. They didn't have anyone who would be disappointed if they failed to push themselves or persevere at some task until they got it right. I didn't insist that they stick to any script, and without Mom making a fuss, what kid is going to work extra-hard? They were allowed to do everything no matter what kind of students they were, and as a result they didn't really try.

Not that either my son or daughter turned out badly. In fact, they turned out amazingly well when you consider what kind of nutcase they had for a mother. But they really had to figure everything out on their own, which is the hard way for a kid. More rules and regulations, more discipline and high expectations, and childhood would have been better. If I had had a more normal home life as a child, maybe my domestic life would have had a chance too. But I didn't, so it didn't.

Robin seemed to handle it well. If she was distressed, she did a good job of hiding it. Jordan, though, let it all out. He was a lovable but impossible kid. A great laugh and a wonderful sense of humor, but a dark side too. Discontented. Intense. His sister saw me as a fun mom who was maybe a little *too* daffy, but no worse than that. Jordan resented the way my illness affected his childhood. I never saw him play ball; we never went on a family vacation; the list went on.

"Where were you brought up?" Robin would ask him when he vented his anger. "You have such pain from this family that I was not privy to."

Not that it was Ozzie and Harriet, of course.

I once told my daughter, "You have me to thank for *your* good marriage."

"What are you talking about?" she asked.

"I showed you everything *not* to do."

My mother loved being negative, I think. It was a way of affirming her vision of herself and her life. As long as she held tight to all the bad things that had come her way, she could justify being so unhappy. But if she had let any light or joy into her life, she would have had no excuse for being so miserable all the time. She would tell the most terrible, sad stories about her life all the time, over and over. Judy and I heard them all our lives. If we called and she was a little sick, we got a story that had us looking up the number for the funeral parlor.

Late in life she lived in a retirement hotel in Miami Beach. She made sure to tell us about all the misery she had to endure there. A beautiful place, right by the beach, and you'd have thought we stuck her in an abandoned warehouse. I called her every Saturday, like clockwork.

"How's the hotel?" I'd ask, girding myself for her cheerful reply.

"It's the worst place I've ever been in my life," she'd say.

"Really?" I'd ask as though I were surprised. "What's wrong?"

"Oh . . . day after day I sit in this lobby. Alone. I talk to no one. Nobody talks to me. I have no friends here. It's a terribly lonely existence. And I miss you girls."

And so on and so forth, every Saturday. You can imagine how much I looked forward to the weekend, knowing I'd have to endure my regular dose of good news from Florida. When Judy telephoned she got the same exact thing. It really got to me after a while, so one day I called Judy and said, "I'm going to surprise Mom and pay her a visit. She sounds so lonesome there, maybe it'll cheer her up."

So I fly to Miami and arrive at the hotel on a Saturday night. Now, usually the lobby was full of yentas chattering away. On this night—deserted. Not even my mother sitting alone in her misery. I go to the front desk and ask, "Can you tell me where Ann Richman is?"

"In the bingo hall," the clerk tells me.

"In the bingo hall," I repeat, dumbfounded.

"She's the bingo caller," she says.

"She's the bingo caller," I say.

"Yes," the clerk says. "Every Saturday night we have bingo in the ballroom and we invite senior citizens from all over Miami Beach."

Had to be another Ann Richman. I race over to the ballroom. And up on the dais, pulling numbers from the tumbler, is my mother. She's holding a microphone, only the thing's practically in her mouth, because she has absolutely no idea how to use it. But she's using it, calling bingo. All I can do is stand there and watch. After a few minutes of that I realize that here, in the back of the room, I'm never going to catch her eye. So I leave my luggage and walk right up the main aisle toward the stage.

"Oh my God, it's my daughter!" my mother exclaims, the microphone at her lips.

I grin as all the old ladies perk up and pay attention.

Then, still over the public address system, I hear:

"Linda, you got so *fat!*"

What could I do? There was no hole for me to hide in. There were too many witnesses for murder. So I kept on smiling, looking at all the yentas staring at me, sizing me up, and I said, "Yep, that's my mom." If anybody else had said what she said I'd have been too shocked to speak. But when you get used to Annie, you're ready for the worst at all times. So I shrugged it off.

"Mom—you're the bingo caller?" I said to her once the game ended.

"Just tonight," she said.

"The lady at the desk said you do this every week."

"She's a lying bitch."

"Mom, why would she lie about that?"

"Go ask her. This is the first time I've ever done it. I haven't been out of my room in months."

And she stuck to her guns too. How can you not hate and admire that kind of determination?

My mother's attitude about my appearance caused me a lot of angst. She was really overweight, but she was full of scorn and loathing for fat people. So she took it out on others. Makes perfect sense, right? I remember watching TV with her once and Shelley Winters came on. "Oh my God!" my mother cried. "*Look* at her!" I wanted to say, "Hey, Mom, look at you!" But I held my tongue, which is just one of the ways my mother and I were different.

When the "Coffee Talk" thing started, she had no idea

what to make of it. *Saturday Night Live* was not meant for her. For one thing, it came on about three hours after her bedtime, and so she had never even seen it until her granddaughter's husband began appearing on it. At that point, though, she became a loyal viewer.

Not that she ever understood a thing she saw on it. Sunday mornings she'd call me and say, "Linda, you looked terrible last night."

"Mom, that's not me, it's Mike."

"Oh, I know, but still—where did you get that sweater?"

"Mom, he's doing a spoof of me. It's supposed to be funny."

"Okay, but do you have to look like that?"

She never quite got it. But that didn't stop her from interpreting the whole thing as me looking lousy in an ugly sweater.

While she was living in Florida, my son-in-law, Mike, made *Wayne's World*, his first big movie. Of course, the proud grandmother-in-law wanted to go, and take her ladyfriends too. So she somehow found an ambulance company that took the whole bunch of them to the theater where the movie was playing.

Later that night she telephoned me at home.

"It's the worst movie I ever saw!" she told me. "It's horrible." That's Annie for you—nothing but sunshine.

A few days after my son was buried, my sister and brother-in-law said they would go down to Florida to tell my mother. I was still in shock, but I had enough presence of mind to realize that she might be worried about how I was holding up. So I decided I'd go too, so she could see I was going to be brave for her sake.

So we get there and we tell her and she's crying and we're crying and that's how it goes. Next day I fly home. Day after that she has a stroke.

I was furious! On top of everything else I was feeling, I was crazed with anger at her! How dare she do this to me? This was the absolute worst moment of my life, a tragedy, a catastrophe beyond which I could not see. I was lying in pieces on the floor, needing every ounce of love and support I could get. This was the time she decides to have a stroke?

At that moment, with absolutely no qualms, I made a decision: I donated my mother to my sister. From that second on, I told Judy, Mom was all hers. I wanted no part of her then or at any time in the future.

"She's never been there for me at any other time in my life," I told Judy, "and she isn't here for me now. So to hell with her. She's your mother, not mine."

For the next six months I never once spoke to my mother, either in person or on the phone. Now, I realize how irrational and unreasonable I was being. I didn't truly blame her for having the stroke. But on the other hand, I really did—all my life, when she *did* have a choice, she had let me down. Now she let me down without choosing to. What exactly was the difference? Felt the same to me. That's how deeply sick our entire relationship was, from start to finish.

Just before my mother died she went into a coma. Judy called and told me, and I dropped everything and raced to Florida to make sure I was there if anything happened one way or the other. Finally she began to stir. She opened her eyes a little, looked up at us, and said this:

"Linda, you got fat!"

Then she closed her eyes, fell back into the coma.

"Judy," I said, turning to my sister, "she did it to us again!"

"No," Judy said. "She did it to *you!*"

Even today, she's with me. Sometimes I walk by a mirror, glance into it, and see not me but my mother. Scares me to death. Or I'll look at my hands and see hers. It got so frightening that I went out and spent way too much money on a diamond bracelet for myself. It's a little on the gaudy side, but there's a reason for that. I wanted something that would sparkle and shine brilliantly, to remind me that even though my mother never thought so, life can be bright and shiny and full of color and light. So now I look down and see hands adorned by gold and diamonds—my hands, not hers.

Or I'll look at my eyes and see hers. Which is why I almost never leave the house without eye makeup, the whole nine yards. It's not that I'm such a cosmetics fiend. It's that otherwise I scare myself to death every time I look in a mirror. Again, it's the difference between making an effort (my way) and not caring at all how you look or seem to the world (her way). Deep down I believe that I could turn into my mother at any moment, so every day I do my best to battle that possibility. You take your motivations where you find them. If I couldn't have a great mother to learn from, then I had to turn my highly dysfunctional mother into a role model in reverse. She taught me how *not* to be, which is an important lesson in itself.

There was something more I took from that whole experience. I know lots of people who aren't on speaking terms with their parents. A lot of them have plenty of good reasons for going incommunicado too. But I think there's a better path, if you can only train yourself to take it. If you've got a mother or a father as screwy as mine was, you've just got to tailor your expectations accordingly. Do you know the saying, you can't get blood from a stone? Well, you can't get sanity and support and acceptance from certain individuals. Doesn't make them worthless. Just means that you can't expect what they don't have to give. So do you cut off all contact now and forever? You don't have to—instead, you can accept whatever good is there and ignore the rest. Go selectively deaf. If you do, maybe things between you will at least relax a little. If you don't, you'll never know if improvement was a possibility. That's not to say you can't take the occasional parent-break when she gets to be too much. I once went three months without seeing my mother, she was getting on my nerves so badly. But after three months we were good as ever, God help me.

3 The Incurable Homebody

Do you think it was coincidence that my adventure in agoraphobia was triggered by a visit to Mom?

Oh, did I somehow fail to mention this? Amazing. She was being treated for severe depression at a private psychiatric hospital. Now, she had always exhibited symptoms of depression, but this time it wasn't lifting as it usually did. This time it was bad, so bad that the doctors prescribed electroshock therapy. I don't recall being particularly upset at this—if it helped, great, and when she was in the hospital I got a break from my responsibility of caring for her. Since at this time I had a three-year-old son and a three-month-old daughter, a little break was not the worst thing in the world.

So on this particular day I jump into a taxi and ride to her hospital, which was maybe two miles from our home, for a visit. I find her in her room staring vacantly at the ceiling, and I sit down, take her hand, and begin talking, as I always do.

And then I suddenly felt funny. For no apparent reason,

my hands went numb. My head went light. I couldn't breathe.

It got scary.

I jumped up, told my mother I had to go, and ran from the room. I bolted down the hallway and out the door to a bank of pay phones. I called my husband, the sweat running down my face, my fingers barely able to dial, my heart pounding and racing like never before.

I was dying and I knew it. I tried explaining it to my husband. Now he was scared, so he told me to call a nurse or a doctor and have them get me to the emergency room. It sounded like I was in the middle of a heart attack.

No, I said, I can't stay in here another second, and I dropped the receiver, ran out the door, and jumped into a cab. If I was gonna die, I was gonna die at home.

When we got to my building I forced the driver to escort me to my apartment, and once I got there I collapsed. A doctor was summoned. He came to the conclusion that I was in a hysterical state—a medical genius!—and injected me with a tranquilizer.

For the next three days, I slept. When I woke up I didn't feel so hot. I was still shaky and weak, and still right on the edge of panic. I felt that way for the next eleven years, during which I never left that apartment.

I mean not once. I was a young wife with two babies when, suddenly, I found it impossible to step out the door. I couldn't even go to the mailbox to get the mail—too close to the outside world. Just the thought of touching the doorknob left me weak with fear. I was certain that if I left, I'd be overcome once again with the dizziness and the racing heart and the faintness. I was sure I'd collapse in the street and die. Given all that, would you leave the house?

Fortunately, at the time we lived in an apartment building in Queens that was filled with young families, so there were plenty of women my age. I made bargains with them as a survival technique. For instance, I had a friend named Carol who hated kids but had two of them. I, on the other hand, love kids, so we made a deal—I'd baby-sit hers while she did the grocery shopping for both of us. I manipulated and maneuvered everyone in that building so I could keep up with my responsibilities without ever stepping outside. Of course, I wasn't a flawless wife and mother during that time. I wasn't out dancing at Studio 54 with my husband. I had to let eleven years' worth of parent-teacher nights and bake sales and school plays go by.

But I survived. There was no name for whatever was wrong with me, and no name was needed. People tended not to dwell on the fact that I never actually went outside, and I was grateful for that. The psychiatrists I consulted said I was neurotic. Everybody else said I was nuts. I said it too—my mother had been pretty crazy, after all, and this, I figured, was just one of those unpleasant inheritances you can end up with, like thick ankles. I got insanity. For a while I decided that I was just eccentric. I embraced that label because it sounded so much more interesting than either neurotic or insane.

There are two aspects of that entire decade-plus from which I take encouragement. First, the fact that it ended. That happened because I was reading an issue of *Redbook* when I came across an article on something they called "agoraphobia." And it told about it, and it gave all the symptoms, and it said that the first major research in the U.S. on this thing was about to start at Long Island Jewish Hospital.

I immediately called the hospital and spoke to the people in charge. I said, "Listen, I have every symptom you

29

describe here, and I'd love to know more about this, but first, can you tell me how to pronounce it?"

They gave me the whole rundown and told me about studies that had been conducted in England on how to cure it, and they invited me to take part in the program here.

"I would love to," I said. "Thank God you're here, what do I have to do?"

"Well, first you have to come to the hospital to be evaluated," they said.

"Wait a second," I said. "You haven't been listening. I've been stuck in this apartment in Queens for eleven years!"

"We know what you mean," the sympathetic voice said. "But there's no way around it. You'll just have to do it."

This taxed even my powers of manipulation and resourcefulness. But I found a way. My friend Carol the kid-hater and I got somebody in the building to watch all four of our kids for a day. Carol would drive me to the hospital and then stay there with me during the intake session. She'd sit in the car in the parking lot, and I'd always be positioned so I could look out a window and see her there. The procedure took seven hours, but she was going to stick it out. She'd eat in the car. If she had to, she'd pee in the car. But she wasn't going to budge. She was going to be my touchstone. Or, more to the point, my lifeboat.

She got me there by coming into my apartment, putting a blanket over my head, and leading me by the hand to her car. I lay down on the floor of the backseat, and she covered me again with the blanket. Then she drove. She walked me into the hospital with the blanket over my head again.

Once there, I was given a battery of physical and psychological tests. At the end of the day they sent me home and said they'd be in touch. Again with the blanket and the floor of the car, and then back home, where I collapsed from exhaustion and remained asleep for the next three days.

Three weeks later I got a call from the hospital saying that I was definitely agoraphobic.

I cried.

"You just made me the happiest woman in the world," I said. As soon as I got off the phone I called everybody I knew and said, "Guess what? I'm not nuts! I'm agoraphobic!"

The hospital also invited me to take part in a ten-week program designed to cure agoraphobia. There were around ten of us in a room for five hours at a shot. Group therapy. This may sound awful, but I didn't really care much about why everybody else in the group was so screwed up. I really thought they were losers and jerks compared to me. I thought their fears were so absurd. One woman there was afraid of fog! Have you ever heard anything more ridiculous?

I would come home and call my sister on the phone and say, "Judy, you wanna laugh?"

It never dawned on me that I sounded just as crazy as they did. I was afraid of the sky! My doorknob gave me chills!

But gradually we began to improve. At one point the doctors decided we were ready for a field trip. You can imagine. Ten adults in sheer terror.

They took us to a Long Island Railroad station. Now, as part of my particular brand of agoraphobia, I was terrified of practically everything, but especially of trains. Don't ask me to explain—none of it makes sense. Just imagining getting on a train made me sweat.

So we all ride together to the train station parking lot. It took me twenty minutes just to get out of the van. I edged toward the little brick station building like I was approaching Dracula's castle. I knew that just around the other side of the building were the tracks. In a few minutes, I sensed, a train would be coming down those tracks.

So I just sat down on the ground and began to cry. Paralyzed with fear. I can't even make it to a bench—too close to the tracks. One of the therapists comes and sits next to me, talking, counseling, advising. But no way in hell am I going to get up off that sidewalk. We spend about an hour there, and then it's time to climb back into the van and head for the safety of the hospital. I never even saw a train that day. I heard one go by, and that was plenty close for me.

Next time, same thing. I was like a tree in that sidewalk. I wasn't going anywhere.

Time after that, a little better—I made it all the way around to the other side of the building, the train side. I shut my eyes and clenched my teeth and had my shoulders up around the top of my hairdo when the train pulled in. But I survived.

Next day we came back. And the day after that too. Before long, I think I just got so sick and tired of coming to the station and trembling that my mind rebelled and I got on the damn train. Whatever part of my brain that feared the train had become numb from all those trips. We *all* got on the train. And we rode it, feeling as though we were the first manned mission to Mars. We rode it all the way into Manhattan, got off, got on another train, and went back to Long Island.

I believe I ultimately got over agoraphobia because I was such a good patient. I always did the homework that the therapists assigned us, even when it hurt.

For instance, they decided that I might benefit if I went to a mall near my house and rode on the escalator. Okay, I said, let's go to the mall.

Of course, I was too terrified to go alone. Not to mention how embarrassed I was to be on escalator therapy. So I always took a bunch of friends or relatives with me. My daughter, who was around ten or so and should have been out playing with her friends, had the job of holding my hand as we rode up and down. Imagine how humiliating that was for me, turning my own precious girl into my handler. I still feel guilty about it.

The worst part was that my mother actually worked in that mall, as a sales clerk at Ohrbach's department store. Now, I had spent eleven years never leaving my house, and my mother still had no idea what was wrong with me. We never even discussed it, if you can believe that. It was just Linda being Linda—meaning crazy—and what more was to be said?

Then, one day, I'm riding down the escalator and who's standing at the bottom?

"I've been watching you for the past hour," she said.

"Uh-huh," I said.

"You've just been riding this escalator."

"Uh-huh."

"Where are you going?"

"Nowhere." Then I got up some nerve. "Everywhere!"

Finally I told my mother the whole thing—I had a disorder with a fancy Greek name, and riding up and down the escalator was supposed to help cure me.

"Hmm!" she said. Meaning: Crazy Linda! But better than anybody else, she knew where I got it.

After that ended, I took my first plane ride ever, to Washington, D.C. Then I started flying everywhere. I became a life junkie. I just felt reborn. That's where I learned one of the most important principles of my life: You can do anything over again. Just spent eleven years stuck inside your apartment? It takes only one step outside and you're ready to start fresh! The do-over was born.

There was another important thing I took from my eleven years of being housebound. A few years into my self-imprisonment, I began to fear that watching daytime TV was making me stupid. Those soap operas were a powerful narcotic, believe me. So once a week I'd send my husband to the library to get me a load of books. Each week I would choose a new subject—modern history, then economics, and so on. I'd go through a book a day, and after a few years of that, believe me, I got quite an education. I had only gone through high school, so this became my private university. I never got a degree, of course, but I am a great resource on any number of subjects. So I taught myself that even in something as devastating as agoraphobia you can create some good. I refuse to waste any experience, no matter how negative it seems at the moment.

The final lesson came from the fact that after just ten weeks of therapy—the blink of an eye—I came out from under eleven years of madness. Agoraphobia ruled my existence, and yet how bad could it have been if in ten short weeks I could get over it? I was partly infuriated—why couldn't I have been cured in Year One of staying home? Why did fate want me to have spent eleven years in that hell?

But the experience proved to me that everything I needed in life was within my grasp. All along I had the power to get over agoraphobia. Therapy had taught me that important lesson. I didn't need somebody else to do it, or a magic wand. I got myself over it, with a little help.

Part of that help, actually, was a magic little pill. When the group therapy sessions started, we all were prescribed a medication that would help us through the rough spots, we were told. We were also warned that the pill had some possible side effects—dry mouth, headaches, diarrhea.

Not long after I started taking it I had to call the hospital and say, "Look, the headaches are killing me. And my mouth is so dry it hurts. And my stomach is feeling funky. Please, can't you give me something to help?"

And they did—they prescribed a second pill to counter the side effects of the first one, and before long the headaches and so on went away.

Then, one year later, we were informed that only half of us had been getting the medication. The rest were getting placebos.

Can you guess which half I was in?

Boy, was that embarrassing. Like an idiot, I was suffering the side effects without ever getting the medicine. But there was a huge lesson in that too, about the power of the human mind—my particular human mind, in this case— to control reality. Of course, such a big lesson doesn't sink in easily. I've gone through lots of situations since then where I failed to exercise all the power I had to make things go my way. I can't emphasize enough though, what a constant refrain this has been in my life—that I am in control, whether I realize it or not.

4 Losing Jordan

It was going to be a hell of a nice day. Tuesday, September 4, 1990, gorgeous weather for summer, and I woke up feeling absolutely fabulous. I decided to go for a walk. On a whim I went into a beauty salon I had never visited before, convinced somehow that I'd get a great haircut there. And lo and behold, I did.

This was maybe the happiest period of my new life. I'd just walked out on the thirty-year mistake that was my marriage. I'd quit my job and started my own business. For a while, money was so tight that I was reduced to shacking up with relatives, a week here and a week there. I stayed longest with my daughter—Robin's boyfriend (now husband), Mike, worked nights, so they'd be going to bed when I was leaving for work, passing like ships in the night. They think I stayed with them for a week; it was more like three months. Finally, I was able to afford a place of my own—the first of my "new" life. Things were looking up, as they say.

Back home on that beautiful September day I raised all

the blinds to let the sun in and opened all the windows. I got some work accomplished. A friend, Richard, came by for a visit. At around four in the afternoon, my doorman buzzed.

"The police are here to see you," he said.

"Uh-oh, they're gonna take me away for traffic tickets," I told Richard, laughing.

I laughed until I opened the door and saw two extremely tall police officers standing there with serious expressions.

"Ma'am, do you have a son named Jordan?" one asked.

"Yes, I do," I said, thinking, *Holy shit, he's been arrested!*

He had turned twenty-nine a week earlier. Thanks to my new good fortune I was even able to send him a check for his birthday, the perfect gift for a starving playwright.

"He was killed in an auto accident this morning," the officer said.

"Impossible!" I said, not missing a beat. "First of all, he never carried his driver's license, so you probably made a mistake on the identification. What kind of car was it?"

"A Mercedes," he said.

"And he never owned a Mercedes," I replied, putting an end to the discussion.

"The car belonged to his employer," the officer said.

"No, there's obviously been some mistake," I said. "Please call the police in Westchester County so I can speak to whoever was at the accident scene."

He dialed the phone and turned it over to me. But the officer there just gave me the same misinformation.

"Okay," I told him, "now I'd like to speak to somebody else there."

Only I didn't know who. Helplessly, I looked at Richard. I was shaking and tears were rolling down my cheeks.

"Richard, this can't *be!*" I said as he took me in his arms.

"Please, please call Judy!" My sister would straighten this out right away.

She was vacationing in Florida at the time. Richard got her on the phone and handed it over to me.

"Jordan was killed in a car accident!" I screamed into the phone. "And I was mad at him for so long!" I have no idea what exactly that meant. But I still remember perfectly the awful sound of my screams. They're still ringing in my head.

"I'll be right there," Judy said, and then she hung up. Of course, I knew how long the trip would take. But the shock of Jordan's death had done something to my brain. It was as if I had lost my footing. Time lost all meaning. So when fifteen minutes had passed and Judy still wasn't with me, I got hysterical.

"Where is she?" I screamed. "Why isn't she here?" No amount of sensible explanation could calm me.

Within an hour I had turned numb, and I stayed that way for quite a while. Either numb or hysterical, that was me over the next few weeks. Like a robot, I did what I had to do. First I called my cousin Barbara and told her the news. She lived in Manhattan, near my daughter.

"Go to Robin's," I instructed her, "so she won't be alone when I tell her what happened. Say you were jogging by her building, so she won't be suspicious. Then call me from there."

She followed my rather sensible plan. "Put Robin on the phone," I told her when she called.

Then, quite steadily, I told my daughter; "Your brother Jordan was killed this morning in a car accident. I think you should pack a suitcase and come here now."

"Okay," she said flatly, and hung up. How bad off was she? She arrived at my apartment in Queens with a suitcase—full of books. No clothes. I told her to pack, but I didn't say what to pack. A mind is a strange thing.

The two of us went numb that day. The words to describe what happened didn't even have meaning. Jordan is dead. Jordan is dead. Jordan-is-dead-Jordan-is-dead Jordanisdead. What? Jordan is dead? How can that be? Oh, Jordan, you dope! Why would you do such a stupid thing?

Barbara's husband, Myron, approached me an hour or so later and said, "Linda, do you want me to make the arrangements?"

I just stared at him. Arrangements? What did that word mean? Was it English?

"For what?" I asked.

"Where do you want Jordan buried?" he said.

My heart started racing. Jordan buried? How can I bury my child? I don't want to do that. "Let's wait for Judy," I finally said.

"No," he said. "We've got to start doing things now."

"Okay," I said. "What do you want to do?"

"Let's call the funeral parlor and arrange with the morgue to release the body," he said.

I went nuts. It never struck me that my poor Jordan had been lying in a morgue all that time. Suddenly I saw him in a freezing cold metal drawer, like on TV.

"Please!" I said to Myron, weeping. "You've got to get him out of there!"

He called the medical examiner's officer and spoke to someone there.

"Linda," he finally said, covering the phone with his hand, "they can't release the body until tomorrow morning."

I grabbed the phone out of his hand and yelled, "I want my son out of there tonight!" The voice on the other end explained that the coroner who had to sign the release wouldn't be back until the morning.

"You loser!" I screamed, interrupting him. I said such harsh things to him that even now I'm a little ashamed of myself. "You work for the state! You're never going anywhere in life! All you wanna do is protect your little pension . . ." On and on like that. To my amazement, he didn't hang up on me. He must have been willing to indulge me in my grief. In fact, he had the coroner call us a little later and explain how state law prevented them from releasing Jordan's body.

At last Judy arrived. I was surrounded by my family and our closest friends. The phone never stopped ringing with condolences. I slid into a corner on the floor, hugging my knees to my chest, a zombie. Robin quietly went off on her own and, unbeknownst to me, began to write her brother's eulogy.

First thing next morning Judy and Barbara prepared to leave. "To make arrangements," they said. There was that word again. Only later did I learn that they had gone to choose a casket for my boy.

Myron and Richard came back from the morgue. "We identified Jordan," Myron said softly, taking my hand. His words hit me like ice water: Somebody who had actually seen my son dead was standing here in front of me, touching me, speaking to me. Finally it was real.

"What did he look like?" I asked.

"Like he was sleeping," Myron said, an answer that gave me no peace whatsoever. I didn't want him to be dead and looking like he was asleep. I wanted him to be asleep, because then he'd wake up. And to be honest, I'm still waiting for Jordan to wake up. It's been almost ten years since he died, but if tomorrow I found out that he had come back to life, I wouldn't be completely surprised. In my head I know he's gone forever, but some other, maybe even stronger part of me isn't buying it. Sometimes I wonder if that part of me is the part that will meet Jordan again someday.

The day passed in a blur, and then it was evening, time to go to the funeral parlor. I was terrified. I remember entering a darkened room. The coffin was at the rear, closed. My first thought was, what kind of coffin is this with all those curves? I'd have chosen something simpler. Maybe I can exchange it. Then it hit me—you can't return a coffin.

I sat on a couch as far as possible from the coffin. Visitors began to come over and pay their respects. I sat there inside my grief, like a cover over me, thinking about what had happened, what and why. Earlier in the day I learned that Jordan wasn't wearing a seat belt when he was killed. The more I thought about that, the madder I got.

"You idiot!" I yelled at the coffin, as though Jordan could hear me. "What the hell was wrong with you? Did you ever in your life do anything right? Your clothes were always a mess, your room was always a mess, and now this! How stupid!"

Two minutes later I was talking with my family and friends, and even making a joke or two. Then I'd go back to yelling at Jordan. As long as I could yell at him, he was with me.

As the funeral parlor was getting ready to close, Judy came to me and said that a rabbi would stay with the coffin all night, in keeping with the tradition. Good, I thought, Jordan won't be alone. Just because he was dead didn't mean I stopped being his mother. I went home and lay sleeplessly in bed, with one phrase hammering my brain over and over: "Jordan is dead, Jordan is dead . . ."

He was in the middle of his crazy life, just as I was in

the middle of mine. Still, we were extremely close. We'd have a slam-down-the-phone fight today, and be hugging tomorrow, the dispute barely remembered.

"You never should have left Dad!" he'd yell at me.

"Mind your own business!" I'd yell back.

He was an adult, but still like a child in some ways—he thought Mommy and Daddy had to stay together forever. Even though when he was little he'd look up at me and say, out of the blue, "You are so miserable with my father."

"Oh, you're crazy," I'd reply. But he knew.

To Jordan, the glass was always half empty. He was funny, too, but even then in a black way. You either cracked up laughing with him or you wanted to run away, his vision of life was so unhappy. Of course, growing up amid an unhappy marriage, with an agoraphobic mother, is enough to depress anybody. I never saw him play ball, he bitterly reminded me, never saw him in a school play, we never took a family vacation.

But he had found a perfect outlet for his demons—the theater. He was a fledgling playwright who had already had one work performed in a workshop at the prestigious Williamstown Playhouse, in Massachusetts. A starving artist, but with big dreams. He was living in a squalid apartment above a warehouse in Pleasantville, near New York, until he was hired as a male au pair by a rich divorcée who needed help with her kids. Mrs. Reese gave him room and board and a salary. And the use of her fancy car too.

"Sounds terrific," I said when he described the job to me, and how it would give him time to work on his plays. "Give me your new phone number so we can get together." That was the last time we spoke.

I had bought a very stylish black suit a few months before Jordan died, and on the morning of his funeral I eyed it closely in the closet. Suddenly I heard his voice in my head: "What, you're gonna play the bereaved mother?" It struck me so funny that I laughed. I pulled out a white suit with black pinstripes and wore that instead. There was no way I could handle sitting down at the mirror and putting on makeup, until I heard Jordan speak again, saying, "C'mon, Mom, you gotta look good for this." So I put on my full face.

At the funeral parlor, Robin decided that she needed to see her brother one last time.

"I'm going to open the coffin," she said.

"I don't know if I can look," I said.

"Do what makes you feel comfortable," she said, and she walked to the coffin and opened the lid. Inside she placed a book, *The Gentle Brother.* One by one Jordan's cousins and friends approached the coffin and put items inside—letters to him, pictures, other mementos.

"It's gonna look like his room in there," I whispered to Judy. "A real junkhouse."

Then the ceremony began. The service was extraordinarily moving to me. Robin's eulogy was beyond beautiful. By the time we got to the cemetery I was numb. Watching the casket lowered into the ground meant nothing to me. Hearing the rabbi's prayer touched me not at all. And then we were on our way back home, to start over.

But first we had to sit shiva. We Jews do nothing but mourn for seven solid days after a loved one dies. It's kind of a funny thing, shiva. Everybody comes out of the woodwork. You get visits from people you haven't seen or spoken to in decades. They come in with the long faces, and the sad words, and sure enough it works like a charm— you're sadder than you ever thought possible! If you weren't already feeling crushed and devastated by grief, shiva would do it to you. You'd cry even if nobody had died.

As rituals go, it's a pretty good one, I think. It allows you to behave like a normal human being under these circumstances. You really do want the world to stop for a little while, in recognition of the terrible thing that's happened. Somehow it wouldn't feel right to wake up the next morning and go on as though nothing had changed. As I've seen over and over, the failure of people to really allow their feelings to run their course is the source of a great deal of unhappiness. People can go for years with feelings bottled up inside them because at some critical moment they didn't allow themselves a few days to get it all out of their systems.

We sat shiva at Judy's house on Long Island, since I had just a small apartment in Queens. I was out of it the whole time. That week, if Judy told me to eat, I ate. Otherwise I forgot. She even had to put the sandwich in my hand, because just asking if I wanted one or what kind I wanted got no sensible response.

And then the seven days were up, and it was time to reacquaint myself with "normal" life, whatever that was, and figure out how to live it with a great big hole in my heart.

Only I wasn't really ready for shiva to end. Maybe I still had more grief to process. Maybe I was too frightened to attempt living in this seriously damaged condition. I announced to Judy that I was going to need a second week of sitting shiva, and that was that. Being an indulgent big sister, she accepted this without an argument. She was aware of how bizarre I was being. But she was willing to go along with me.

Of course, she was the only one who was. I sat shiva for that entire second week and got not one visitor. Which was fine by me—I didn't require everybody else to overturn centuries of Jewish tradition. But by the end of the second week, I knew this sitting and mourning had run its course. I knew I had pushed it pretty much to the limit.

When that week ended I told Judy I was going back to my apartment.

"Why not stay?" she asked.

"I have to clean," I replied.

I was living in a studio apartment then. I am a thorough cleaner, and it usually took no more than one hour to do the place top to bottom until it shined.

But this was an unusual time. I tore into that apartment like a woman possessed. I removed fixtures that I normally just cleaned around. I pulled down everything, including the blinds and the curtains. I moved every piece of furniture, no matter how big and cumbersome. I used ammonia on the walls and Lysol on the chairs. I had a screwdriver in my pocket, and if anything had screws in it, it got unscrewed so I could clean it from the inside out. First I cleaned the dust and dirt, and when the apartment was clean, I cleaned the clean. I was waging chemical warfare against anything that lived there, myself excluded, and when I was done, that place sparkled. I mean, it was blinding.

I imagine there was some purpose to that orgy of cleaning. I was scrubbing my life down to the bones. I was clearing away everything except for me. You could also just say that I was looking for a physical workout so hard that it would leave me exhausted and unable to think about what had just happened.

Luckily, my friend Richard made it his mission to hang around with me during this period. Just having a normal human being in the general vicinity can mean a great deal. Richard loved movies, so he dragged me along to a lot of pictures. I was grateful for even a few minutes of absorption in somebody else's troubles.

A friend of Richard's, a woman named Susie, invited us both over for Rosh Hashanah, the Jewish New Year. When you lose a child you're not supposed to do anything social for one year, but fortunately I was such a wayward Jew that I had no idea. So we accepted the invitation.

At the last second, though, I decided to stay home. I really didn't feel up to a houseful of people celebrating a holiday. And Susie is Greek, so her family is large and boisterous and lively.

But Richard twisted my arm and we went. Susie took me around the room and introduced me to her relatives one by one, saying, "This is Linda, she's the woman who just lost a son, so try to be understanding."

Now, you may look at that and say, "What a terrible, tactless thing to do to a person!"

But the fact is, it was the best thing anybody had ever done for me.

When you lose a child, people don't know how to act. It makes them extremely uncomfortable. I had old and dear friends who stopped calling me altogether once Jordan died. It was more than they could handle, which is kind of funny when you remember that it wasn't their son who died, it was mine. If I could try my best to handle it, they could make a little effort too, you'd think. But it didn't work that way. People don't know what they're supposed to do— mention it, not mention it, make a big deal, try to ignore it.

Susie didn't mess around. She put it right out there for everyone to see. Imagine meeting a person for the first time and that's the introduction you get. It cuts right through all the usual awkwardness, doesn't it?

It did for me. I felt totally liberated by what Susie was

saying. I didn't have to pretend or explain. If I felt like going off by myself for a few minutes, nobody had to wonder why or whisper about it. They all knew why. There was no pretending.

Best of all, I didn't have to answer what is still a dreaded question: "How many children do you have?"

My palms still sweat waiting for that question to come up. My heart races when I sense it forming. If you catch me off guard, I'll say something like, "You're gonna regret you asked me that. I had a daughter and a son, and my son was killed in an automobile accident in . . ." That's the long answer, the honest and awkward answer.

Look, I can't just say "Two" and leave it at that, can I? No way.

I can't say "One" either. That would be technically true, though I am the mother of two children, even now. I'd like to say, forthrightly, "I have two children, a daughter and a son who's dead." But even I have limits to what I'll say to unsuspecting strangers. Here's what I usually end up saying: "I have one in heaven and one on earth." It gets the point across without too much distress.

We buried my son in a cemetery in Queens. When I went there to arrange for the grave I decided to ask about mausoleums, having no idea how much they cost. (Little did I know we were talking a million-dollar-plus price tag for the plot plus construction.) So I find the cemetery manager and we're talking. My sister cannot handle conversations of any kind about death, so she's rushing me and pinching me to finish.

"Judy," I said, "would you rather not be here for this conversation?"

"Just hurry it up," she said.

"Look, you're gonna die someday, so we might as well

all end up together," I tried to reason with her. But she wasn't hearing me.

The guy is trying to show me something on a map.

"Do you want to be here?" he said. "This is near the Streisand family mausoleum."

"I beg your pardon?" I said.

"The Streisand family has a mausoleum in this area of the cemetery."

That's all Judy had to hear. "We are leaving *now!*" she said, grabbing my arm.

"Hold on!" I said. "I wanna live near the Streisands!"

"Now!" she said, exiting the office. We were laughing *and* crying.

We buried Jordan in that cemetery, though not in a mausoleum. I kind of dread going there to visit, though I do it every time I'm in New York, and in fact, I had a tough time moving away from New York because I felt as though I was abandoning my son. Luckily, he's buried in a grave with my Aunt Pat, so I know at least he's got company.

5 | The First Laugh Is the Hardest

This was maybe three weeks after my son was killed.

I was in agony. I was so devastated, I was in shock. A zombie. If you spent two seconds in a room with me you knew you were looking at a basket case.

On this particular day I was with my daughter. Also in shock. But she and I run at different temperatures, emotionally speaking. She's reserved and private with her feelings. I'm out there.

I look at her and it's clear that she's suffering terribly this day. She's actually crying, tears coming down her face but without a sound.

Why is she in such pain at this particular moment? From seeing me, her mother, in agony. It's funny—we were both suffering due to the same terrible event, but we tried our best to protect each other from the pain. You feel guilty letting someone who loves you see how bad you feel.

Anyway, I look at her and realize that I'm the one making her suffer so. This was the first moment since Jordan died that any other thought sunk all the way into my mind.

I was making my daughter suffer, and I decided I had to stop it at once. "Decided" is the key word—I made it my business to take control of this particular minute.

"You think you're sad?" I said to her. She looked up.

"When your brother died he owed me a lot of money," I moaned. "And now I'll never see a dime!"

Robin stared at me. And then she giggled.

She didn't giggle. It was smaller than that—a gigglet.

But it stopped her crying. It was as close to a laugh as either one of us had gotten for three weeks.

It was a sign.

Of what? That I still had a sick sense of humor and could joke about completely inappropriate things? I guess it was. But it was also a reminder, for both of us, that someday we would laugh again. Not right away. Someday.

And what was the significance of that? Well, no matter how sad you are, you know that you will eat again. And drink. You'll go on breathing and walking and talking. At some point you'll have to shop again, even if only for necessities. In other words, life—or at least many of the activities that it involves—will go on.

But so what? Is that such a great thing? When you're that sad, you easily imagine that life will go on but you'll go through it like a zombie, in misery and pain and depression for the rest of your days.

Laughter, though—that's something else. If you think that someday you'll laugh again, then you have to accept that someday you'll be happy too. Maybe even joyous. Perhaps you'll sing. Dance. Play the piano.

Anyway, on the day I'm talking about I wasn't looking for a sign of anything. I just knew that my daughter was in pain and I had to stop it, if only for a moment. I tried in the only way I knew how—I made a joke.

There are times when making a joke is the difference between life and death.

A friend of mine and his wife had been trying unsuccessfully to have a child. They ended up at a very expensive weekend workshop at Harvard University for couples in their predicament. The first day of the workshop was all about fallopian tubes and egg cells and sperm cells and all that jazz. The second day the experts discussed laughter and how it can release the endorphins and other stuff in your body that will maybe allow you to relax enough to conceive.

I was amazed when I heard that. Even Harvard now acknowledges that laughter can do things medical science can't.

A young man came to one of my seminars and then approached me when it was done. He was born into a Hasidic Jewish family but could no longer live that exacting religious lifestyle. As a result, his parents ostracized him— they would no longer have anything to do with him. He lost his business too. He had a nervous breakdown. He attempted suicide twice and ended up in a psychiatric hospital. By the time we met he was under the care of a good shrink and no longer wanted to kill himself, so he was on his way back from the brink.

But he was still in pretty sad shape. After my lecture, he told me that for the first time in his ordeal he had hope about how his future might turn out. Of course I was flattered, so I asked why.

"Well," he told me, "you've been through your own personal holocaust, but now you seem fine."

"Do you know what fine means?" I asked him. "It means Fucked up, Insecure, Nervous, and Emotional. And you're right—I *am* F.I.N.E.!"

He laughed, which made his day and mine.

A young woman found me after another lecture. She had lost a daughter, nine years old, to a brain aneurysm. Unheard of. Shocking. She went into a depression so deep that she too had attempted suicide. And she was also in and out of mental hospitals.

"Tonight you made me embarrassed at myself," she told me.

"What are you talking about?" I said. "Never do that to yourself. Never be embarrassed."

"But with all you've suffered, you're whole now," she said. "And I want to be whole too."

I'm not supposed to meet with people from my lectures one-on-one, because I have no credentials. But I said, "Screw this, let's meet later in the TV room."

We sat and talked for a long time about our shared experiences and how crazy you feel in the first year after you lose a child—about the ups and downs of the roller-coaster. One minute you feel fine, and then the next minute you're not fine, and then you're fine, and then you feel bad because you're fine, and then you're not fine. That's exactly how it goes—the second you start to feel okay you feel guilty about it. And that was very meaningful for her, because she realized that that cycle was a big part of what was keeping her down. How are you ever going to feel good if feeling good makes you feel guilty?

So we talked, and somehow in all that talking we brought up the extreme things people do under the influence of grief. I told her about my need to stop strangers on the street and tell them that my son died.

And she said, "What?"

"Oh, *yeah,*" I told her. In the first year after my son died, I got into the habit of telling total strangers all about it. I'd be in the supermarket checkout line, for instance, and the person in front of me would glance at the rack of tabloids and remark, "Oh, look, Oprah's gained weight again."

To which I would reply, "My son died in an automobile collision."

They'd go, ". . . Excuse me?" And they'd kind of slink away and get the hell out of that supermarket as fast as possible. Back then I used to take buses just so I would have a captive audience for my little announcement. I figured it wouldn't affect their lives at all, except that they'd go home and tell everybody about this pathetic crazy woman they met. I would get on the bus with a destination in mind—I lived in Queens then, so I'd say to myself, "Today I'm going into Manhattan." But I knew my real goal was to spend forty-five minutes sitting next to some poor sucker who was about to have his or her mind blown.

We'd start talking the way people do, and he or she might say, "Boy, what a nice day, isn't it?"

Bingo. "My son just died."

It was an impulse. I couldn't resist it. I'd get onto the bus knowing I'd do it. But still I got on. It was wacky, but telling strangers actually did make me feel less anxious. Maybe it made the people I told *more* anxious, but I didn't care.

Anyway, I was telling this woman who had lost her nine-year-old about my crazy year just to let her know that she wasn't the only one. I wanted her to know why she shouldn't be embarrassed, because in her position I was a total nut! Imagine the absurdity of it—this nice little depressed lady from Queens would get on a bus every day and shock people out of their shoes. You go out in the morning with a plan to destroy somebody's day, and it makes you feel good! It's crazy. But it's funny too. You can't imagine the faces on these people as they looked around for the emergency exit. I think people actually moved out of Queens because of me.

So I'm telling her all this, and her response is what you'd expect: She's howling. I mean, she's laughing hysterically.

Now, she wasn't laughing at the death of my child. I wasn't asking her to find something funny in that. It's not a joke. She wasn't laughing at my sadness. A broken heart's not funny. But we were both laughing at how we human beings react to horror. Sometimes that can be very funny. And finding something funny—anything—under those painful conditions is good. If you can laugh even while you feel pain, there's hope.

"But how do you stop feeling the pain?" she asked me once she stopped laughing.

"You don't," I said.

You have to integrate the pain into your life, I told her. It doesn't go away. It can't. It shouldn't. It's part of you. You had a beautiful little child and now you don't. That loss is part of you, just like your daughter was. These feelings are your feelings. What happened to you was hideous and horrible, and now you have to find a way to go on and even to rediscover laughter and joy. It doesn't even matter what you laugh at. If you give yourself time, and if you try a little, you'll find that first laugh. That gigglet. It comes, eventually, if you stick around for it.

My sister Judy and I are extremely close to our cousin Barbara. One day Barbara called to say she found a lump in her breast and was going into the hospital for tests.

"Judy, how awful, Barbara has cancer," I told my sister on the phone.

"What do you mean, cancer? All she knows so far is that she has a lump," my sister replied.

"Well," I said, "she's under a lot of stress, and when you can't let it out sometimes it attacks you." Now, I realize that genes and environment are the big causes behind cancer. Still, to this day I believe she would have avoided a lot of sickness had she only banished the stress from her life. That's why the subject of emotional and spiritual health is so important to me. It's not just about feeling calm or going through life with a song in your heart. If you don't have a healthy inner life, you are going to suffer physical illness. Maybe even something fatal, if you're not careful.

Anyway, she had the tests, and sure enough, it *was* cancer. She's going to have a double mastectomy and she insists on having reconstructive surgery done at the same time. She's a thin woman, so they'll have to remove tissue from her back in order to build her new breasts, a fourteen-hour procedure altogether. Naturally, Judy and I are there at the hospital the whole time, start to finish.

When it's over the doctor comes out and tells us that she's fine, the surgery was a success, she's in the intensive care unit because it was such a long ordeal. We can't see her right away, but if we come back the next day we can visit.

Fine, we tell him, and he leaves.

"Okay, I'm going in," I tell my sister.

"Didn't you just hear the doctor?" she asks.

"What are they gonna do, put me in visitor jail?" I reply. I begin looking around for a white lab coat I can borrow, just in case, and when I find one I slip it on and stride in a purposeful way into the ICU.

There I find Barbara in her bed, hooked up to a million tubes and wires and gadgets. For some reason, they've left her breasts uncovered. So the first thing I do is take the sheet and gently bring it up to her chin.

"Barbara," I whisper into her ear. "Your boobs look beautiful." I let that sink in. "But now your face looks like shit! You need a facelift!"

In response I hear this quiet, breathy little "Heh-heh-heh . . ."

Look, if under those conditions somebody joked about *your* new boobs, you'd take that as a sign you were probably doing all right. When I tried to be funny, she got the message. As long as we were laughing, she knew she was going to survive.

Over the next few days she had a steady stream of visitors, most of whom would say things like, "Oh, look at you! Barbara, your color's great!"

To which I would say, "What are you talking about? She's gray! She's dead!"

She was the one in stitches, but we were both laughing. Of course, I would never talk that way about a stranger. This is the kind of tender, loving treatment I reserve for family and close friends only.

6 How to Throw a Pity Party

People think that because I have endured a lot of pain I will have a great deal to say on the subject, including a few words of magic healing.

They're out of luck.

Here's all I know about pain: Nobody wants any, and everybody gets some. That's all anybody knows about pain right there in one little sentence.

You sure don't want any, am I correct? And no wonder! Pain hurts.

The people around you don't want you to have any either, because even watching somebody in pain is painful. When you've suffered some horrible loss, your loved ones will tell you to be brave and strong. Whereas, if it was *your* welfare they had in mind, they'd tell you to be scared and weak. Because pain is scary, and in the grip of it we're all weak. Scared and weak makes perfect sense.

If it was you they were thinking about, they'd tell you to scream and cry and fall apart and claw at the carpet and foam at the mouth and faint dead away. They'd tell you to crawl under the dining room table and curl up in a ball and stay there.

That's what you're supposed to do when you're in big pain. That's normal.

Even if they didn't tell you to be brave and strong, you know that's what they hope you'll do. You know that because you've been there yourself, telling *them* to be brave and strong. We even tell ourselves to be brave and strong. I remember when the police officers came to my house to tell me my son had been killed. They made their little announcement, and then, when they were through, I offered to make coffee. My brain blocked out reality and put me on autopilot.

In one of my workshops at Canyon Ranch, a woman whose teenage son had died in a car crash told almost the same story—when the cops informed her the boy had been killed, she heard her own voice say, "Gee, it must be really hard on you guys, having to deliver this kind of news." Cuckoo. But it's the way we all operate. Put off the pain. Deny it. Cancel it if you can.

Of course, you can't. All you can do is delay it. Which is the worst thing you can do, because then it festers. It grows huge and ugly. It builds up pressure and power. In the end, delaying it means you have more pain to deal with, not less. Because, sooner or later, the pain finally breaks through all the defenses and settles in for a good, long siege. That pain has no other plans for the foreseeable future. It unpacks its bags and prepares for a lengthy visit.

"When does the pain finally pass?" people ask me.

"It doesn't," I say.

"No, seriously," they say.

"I'm serious," I reply.

"Never?" they ask.

"Never," I answer.

They wait for the rest of the wisdom. Some of them are still waiting.

Look, I tell them, I know it sucks. But that's the way it is. You want me to tell you how to get rid of the pain. But nobody can tell you that. If someone tells you she can, run away fast. If your thumb came off you'd cry. What makes you think that if you lose a child, or a love, or a dream, it's not going to hurt? In fact, by wanting to be pain-free, you're devoting all your energy and efforts to something that is doomed to fail. You're ducking reality. Which makes it impossible to learn to live with it.

When my son died, first I was numb, but then the pain set in. When it did, I was like an animal caught in a steel trap. I was crazy with pain. It was physical and mental and emotional and spiritual and anything else you can think of. I wasn't *in* pain—I *was* pain. If there was a secret word to get rid of it, I would have found it. I certainly searched for it high and low—I went to 103 lectures in one year looking for the answer. If there was a pill for my pain, I would have taken it in a heartbeat.

I look at it this way: If I didn't love my son, it wouldn't have hurt to lose him. You're supposed to hurt when you lose someone you love. That is just the natural order of things, and although I am no great admirer of the natural order of things, I have learned by now that you don't screw around with it. You accept it or drive yourself nuts. The pain of losing my son was equal to the joy of having him. When he was born it was extremely joyous—my first child. When he died, the pain was just as extreme.

I spent years going around and around on this, on trying to digest or absorb or cure or heal the pain. Anything to stop feeling so much of it. In the end, here's what I realized: I hurt because my son died. So in not wanting any

61

more pain, what I really wanted was to go back in time and make that terrible thing un-happen. That's what I needed—nothing less would do.

Once I accepted that my wish would never come true, which took a very long time, I accepted the pain. That was the moment I knew that pain and I were going to be together for as long as I live.

At that point, the pain began to dim.

Boy, ain't that a kick in the head? You have to take that goddamn pain, that terrible, terrible enemy, and treat it like your partner. Like your mate. You have to love that ache, the actual feeling of it, before you can begin learning to live with it. I will always have the pain of losing my son. But it will never again feel as it did when the loss was fresh. Back then it burned like the fires of hell. Today it's a dull throb—always with me, but manageable for the most part.

I say manageable because for all my insistence that you can't do much to get rid of the pain, you can control it.

People ask me, "When the pain gets too hard to bear, how do you fight it?"

"I don't," I say.

"You don't?"

"I give in," I tell them.

"You what?"

"I give in," I say.

If I wake up and feel down and sad and depressed, I explain, I cancel everything for the next day or so. I don't take a shower, and I don't wash my hair. I don't even leave my bed except when nature requires me to. I grab two bags of potato chips, I pull the covers over my head, and I lie there feeling sorry for myself. I weep. I curse. I suffer—not just a little. A lot. I suffer as much as is humanly possible. I suffer more in two days than most people do in a year. I do everything I can to make myself feel as bad and sad as possible.

Nobody throws a pity party like I do.

"And then what happens?" they ask.

"On the third day," I tell them, "I get up."

"You get up."

On the third day, I say, whether I want to or not, I get out of bed, I take a shower, I wash my hair, I put on makeup and get the hell out of the house. That's the key to the whole thing. That's my brilliant solution. You allow yourself to behave like an insane person for exactly two days. Two days is healthy. Two days is *healing*.

Three days is dangerous.

Two days is a beneficial method of dealing with your pain so you can get over it a little. Three days is a running start on the road to agoraphobia—take it from someone who's been there and done that. So on the third day, like Jesus Christ, you get up, get dressed, get going.

"Huh!" they say. Sometimes their mouths hang open a little.

It sounds like the worst advice any sad person has ever gotten, doesn't it? It sounds like a good excuse to let your troubles turn you into a zombie. But it has the opposite effect. Rather than spend every day feeling halfway undone by sadness and depression, rather than go through life always feeling gloomy and preoccupied by loss, I pack most of my suffering into just a few days. Those pity parties have an amazingly positive influence on the rest of my life. I always leave those parties feeling great.

The idea for pity parties came to me from something I learned during the therapy that cured my agoraphobia. The shrinks told us that if we wanted to conquer our fears, we had to flood our emotions with them. Instead of protecting ourselves from anxiety—which is a natural impulse, isn't it?—we had to practically bathe in it. Because you can't live in extreme terror all the time. Your mind just can't operate that way.

I use the same general principle at my pity parties. There are certain days of the year when I really feel the sadness and pain of losing Jordan most sharply. On those days, I don't try to fight it. I don't tell myself to be brave and strong and responsible. I just give in. I bathe my brain in pity.

But you really have to do it right. You have to suffer like nobody ever suffered. A few sniffles and some staring out the window won't do it. You've got to drop the bomb on yourself. You've got to scorch the earth.

For instance, as I'm writing this we've just passed Mother's Day. A very bad day in my calendar. Like the second worst day of the year (the worst is the anniversary of my son's death). Mother's Day reminds me of what I no longer have (though I have a beautiful daughter still). On Mother's Day I feel lousy without even trying. Plus, I know that if I attempt to be brave and go about my normal routine I'm going to see a hundred signs announcing Mother's Day brunch and Mother's Day cards and Mother's Day flowers and Mother's Day wrestling matches and at least a dozen numbskulls will as a simple reflex action wish me a happy Mother's Day.

Do I need that?

So here's what I did. I stayed in bed. I didn't take a shower or wash my hair. I grabbed a bag of potato chips and ate it with the covers over my head. And I cried. A whole lot.

On Mother's Day the people who are closest to me know what I'm doing. But they like to call anyway, just to reach out and touch and say they understand.

Don't bother, I order them. The last thing I need to hear

is The Voice. You know the one, where they say, "Linda. How are you holding up?" but in a voice they never use at any other time. Like they're practicing to be undertakers, or maybe they just think that if they make the wrong noise I'll burst into tears and then they'll really wish they hadn't called.

"I don't want to hear The Voice," I tell them. "Call me tomorrow."

So I isolated myself completely. But did I stop there? No way—that's just scratching the surface. In preparation for Mother's Day, I went to the video store on Saturday and rented two movies: *Terms of Endearment* and *An Affair to Remember.*

Now, in the annals of tearjerkers about losing a child, there is no movie to match *Terms of Endearment.* People who have never lost a child weep uncontrollably. People who have never *had* a child weep uncontrollably. It's like the nuclear weapon of dead children cinema.

I've watched it a thousand times.

On that Mother's Day I watched it all the way through just to make sure I was as sad as I could possibly be. But even that didn't do the trick. How did I know it didn't do the trick? I still had some tears left in me. I didn't want to leave one tear unshed.

One of the real gut-wrencher scenes is when Debra Winger's lying in her hospital bed, and the end is near, and Shirley MacLaine, who plays the mother, is screaming at the nurses, "She needs something for the pain! You said you'd give it to her at ten o'clock! It's ten o'clock!" This is where Shirley, who's really held it all together up to this point, begins to experience a total meltdown. She's been brave and strong, and here is where she comes apart at the seams. She implodes with grief and rage. It's something special to watch.

And if you yourself have had a child die in the prime of life? Oh, that scene is ecstasy. That scene causes you the most exquisite agony anybody has ever felt while lying in bed watching a movie. On Mother's Day, after the movie ended, I hit rewind and found the scene. And played it again. And hit rewind. And played it again. And hit rewind. And played it again. After maybe half a dozen times, I was numb from the neck up. I couldn't even be sure I was breathing.

But there were still a few tears left inside my head. So I switched to *An Affair to Remember,* my all-time romantic tearjerker. If you know the movie, you know how powerful the scene is where Deborah Kerr has to give Cary Grant the brush-off without letting him know the real reason— she is crippled from the waist down, and so, as these movies went in the good old days, was an unsuitable wife for him. First I watched the entire movie. Then I watched the big scene, over and over again. By the time I stopped, the scene no longer even made sense to me. I couldn't figure out what the hell was happening. It's like when you repeat a word over and over and the sound no longer makes sense to you. Same thing.

By now my eyes looked like I had just gone twelve rounds with Mike Tyson. My nose was bright red. The bed was damp there were so many soggy tissues. Every breath had to sneak past my swollen sinuses. I looked all around and started to laugh. Partly because it really was a funny sight. But also because, finally, I was physically incapable of sobbing another sob.

You know how some people laugh till they cry? I cry till I laugh.

And on Monday morning I woke up, got dressed, and went out to face the day. I felt pretty damn good too.

You've got to accept pain. You've got to accept it for yourself, and you've got to accept that other people are going to feel it too. You can't spare them, no matter how much you love them, no matter how big the pain is. Everybody has to feel her own pain.

When I was eight years old my father died and my family decided not to tell me. Were they playing a trick on me? No. They were trying to spare a little girl the pain of losing her daddy. It was an insane thing for them to do. For about twenty-five years I wanted to beat the shit out of all of them. Now I accept their reasons for doing it.

But did they spare me pain? Not on your life. In fact, just the opposite happened. They caused me even more pain. If I had lost my father and been allowed to know and acknowledge and feel it, I would have screamed and cried and trembled with fear. I would have been in emotional shock. But at some point I would have absorbed the shock and gotten on with my life.

Instead, my father simply vanished. I had no idea where. Nobody told me, and I was afraid to ask. Something devastating had happened to my life, I knew that much. But I could not say what, and nobody would help me.

You want to talk about pain?

So they did me no favors.

Another good example, from one of my workshops: A very dear woman and loyal Canyon Rancher in her late sixties. Total bundle of energy and good vibrations—the happiest, sunniest person you ever want to meet, which to me automatically triggers alarm bells. Sometimes this is the kind of person who's making a huge effort to seem so happy. You've got to admire people like that. But you've got to learn to listen to them too.

We're in the workshop, maybe eight women in a small group.

Suddenly, out of nowhere, she begins to tell how thirty-five years ago she had a baby die four days after it was

born. The infant came out in trouble and was whisked away
to intensive care, where it lingered until it died. Poor child
was born perfectly formed, beautiful, but damaged inside
somehow. They never let her see the baby that whole time.
They just came in after it was over, told her it was dead,
and buried the body.

The woman is telling this as though it's the first time
she's ever told it. For all I know, it is.

"And you know," she said in this crumpled voice, "they
never even let me name her . . ."

Oh Jesus, we all thought. How awful. You can just imagine the birth certificate—the cold words "Baby Girl" where
the first name should have been. Those were hard-hearted
days back then. Barbaric.

And of course, she was expected to accept all the usual
platitudes—"The child is better off now, she's at peace, it's
God's will." You know the heartless bull as well as I do.

By the time she was finished telling all this, I had my
arms around her, but I really was at a loss. How do you
comfort somebody at this dreadful moment? What do you
say once they've said their piece?

"Did you have a name ready for her?" I asked.

"Oh, yes," she said. "We were going to call her Wendy."

"Okay," I said. "We're going to name that baby today."

By this point we were all sitting on the floor in a small
circle, crying our eyes out.

"Let's all grab a balloon," I said. I realize now how ridiculous this might sound, but at all my workshops I have he-
lium balloons. It's part of the festive, childlike atmosphere
I try to create. Today the balloons were going to serve a
different purpose.

We took the balloons and stepped outside the meeting
room, onto a grassy lawn under some trees.

"Okay," I said. "Let's send these up to Wendy."

And we let go of those balloons. And called hello to Wendy.

Can you tell how absolutely wracked we all were by this? I mean, it was as if we had all lost that child so long ago.

I felt in my heart that I was doing the right thing by this poor woman. That this crazy little naming ceremony I concocted was going to do more good than harm. But part of me was worried that maybe I was unwise to have let so many feelings out without a trained psychologist around to help this woman deal with the next few days.

On Sunday, somebody who works at the Ranch saw me and said, "I heard about what happened yesterday."

"What happened?" I said, holding my breath.

"Oh, about the baby-naming ceremony. That woman is a different person today. She's telling everybody all about it."

Then I ran into the woman.

"Oh, you have no idea what you did to my life," she gushed. "I am at peace. My baby finally has a name. I feel like such a load has been lifted."

The load was all that grief she had been carrying around, unexpressed and unacknowledged, for more than thirty years.

I learned this lesson again recently, in a small, relatively harmless way, thank God.

I was in London with my girlfriend Ellen, and we were shopping in this tiny little boutique. She went into the dressing room, tried on a blouse, and emerged to get a good look. There was no point in taking her things from the dressing room with her, because the store was so small that it was impossible for someone to go in there without us seeing.

She decided to take the blouse, went back to the dressing room for her coat, and discovered that her wallet was gone. Somehow, someone had gotten in there right under our noses.

And she was really upset.

"Oh my God, not just my money, but my passport, my license, my credit cards—everything!" she said.

I, being a good friend, immediately began to try to ease her worry.

"Oh, honey, look, it's only a wallet. Nothing irreplaceable was lost. It's just—"

"Could you please let me be upset for a while?" she said.

Uh-oh—I was wrong wrong wrong, and I knew it the second she opened her mouth. She felt what she felt. And who the hell was I to tell her not to feel it? *It was her wallet.* Bingo. Even *I* know when to shut up.

MY ALL-TIME FAVORITE
TEAR-JERKER MOVIES

1. *Terms of Endearment.* The absolute best.
2. *Schindler's List*
3. *Madame X*
4. *Il Postino*
5. *Life Is Beautiful*
6. *Beaches*
7. *The Way We Were*
8. *An Affair to Remember*
9. *Imitation of Life*
10. *A Star Is Born* (any version)

7 Try It, It Works for Me: Creative Catastrophizing

Here's the entire principle behind the pity party: If you're going to feel lousy anyway, you should feel extremely lousy. You should feel lousier than anybody's ever felt before. You should wring every drop of lousiness out of yourself. Because if you don't, you're going to go through life carrying that lump of lousiness around inside you. It's going to affect you every single minute. There's just going to be this constant stream of sadness and depression and anxiety flowing through your veins, just like those little time-controlled Dristan capsules used to work in the commercials.

Look—what happens when you feel lousy and somebody tells you to cheer up? It makes you feel even lousier. So fighting that sadness—which, again, is what everybody who has to look at your depressing face will advise you to do— is useless. It doesn't work.

Making yourself really and truly sad works like a charm, however. Believe me, you can drive yourself into the absolute depth of despair and hopelessness. And somehow, when you do that, it makes you feel better. It makes no sense at all, and yet it is true. It's like how judo works (not that I know anything about judo, but so I've been told): You take your opponent's momentum and use it against him. If he throws a punch, you don't block it— you get out of the way and let the force of the punch carry him all the way onto his tucchus. If you start out feeling sad, you don't fight it—instead, you make yourself even sadder, and before you know it sadness is flat on its ass and you're walking away whistling a happy tune.

Okay, maybe not a happy tune, but something. Streisand?

Here's an example from my own life. It will sound trivial, but that's the point—it doesn't have to be anything major that sets you off.

I have a coworker at the Ranch who is, to put it politely, the bane of my existence. She doesn't interfere all that much, to be honest, because I know how to neutralize her negativity and knock her down a peg or two when the need arises. I even enjoy it, I have to admit, much as I dislike having any kind of battle ruin my good time.

Once in a while though, she gets on my nerves.

On the day in question, we had a little run-in. And during it, I allowed her to speak to me in a snotty and condescending way. She took great delight in that, I could tell even at the time. But for whatever reason, I was powerless to put her in her place on the spot. Maybe I was having an off day. Whatever—doesn't matter.

Two o'clock in the morning, for no discernible reason, I wake up. I'm lying there, staring at the ceiling, and what's going through my head? The nasty encounter with this rotten bitch. And it's gnawing at me. I allowed her to treat me with disrespect, and I didn't say or do a thing in my own defense. It's eating at me like a weasel. My stomach's churning, and I'm so mad my face feels hot.

I finally fall back asleep, but it's one of those sleeps that doesn't feel like rest. So when dawn arrives and I wake up for good, I'm exhausted. And I'm still full of bile over what happened.

A perfect day for pity.

I start by staring in the mirror. Due to such a fitful sleep, I look like shit. Big bags under my eyes. Sallow skin. Greasy hair. I'm ugly. I'm fat. I'm the fattest, ugliest person in the world. One look at me tells you that I'm the biggest, ugliest loser idiot in the world. Totally worthless.

Which is what I must be, right? What other kind of person allows somebody to talk to them the way I let that woman talk to me? I must be the biggest doormat in the world. I have no ability to stand up for myself or defend myself or battle the bullies out there. I am the patsy and stooge of all time. Whenever this woman or anyone else wants to belittle me or abuse me or make my life miserable, they're going to do so. I'll just have to get used to it.

Because, after all, I am an idiot! A dope! A fool! I must be the most brainless person in Tucson, Arizona! Who else would deserve such treatment? All my life, come to think of it, I have been a dumb jackass who is incapable of doing anything right. Of all the dummies and imbeciles I know, I am the dumbest and most imbecilic.

Well, at about this moment, I laughed right in my own face.

What else could I do? Granted, I started out feeling dumb, but the portrait I painted was clearly an exaggeration, even to a dope like me. And why was I feeling so lousy and subjecting myself to so much insult and injury? Because of that no-good bitch, my coworker. The more I thought about that, the angrier I became. The nerve of her, trying to make me feel bad. And what made her think she can get away with it? Hey, I've overcome genuinely terrifying obstacles in my life. I've built success from nothing, from the ground up. Next to that, what has she ever done? Nothing. Not a thing.

I stared back in that mirror, and the air turned blue with the obscenities and profanities I hurled at her. Before long I felt the strength of ten pissed-off Jewish women from Queens, New York, where even a single pissed-off Jewish woman is something before whom all others tremble!

Now I was laughing again. And feeling much better. I had gotten myself from frustration to despair to rage to laughter in less than an hour. At that point I was ready to face the world, which is exactly what I did.

Here's another example. I have a cousin who has an only child, a daughter, and they are enmeshed and intertwined beyond my ability to describe. You know how mothers and daughters can be. These two are way caught up in each other. Which is not necessarily a bad thing, though it can be, as any mother or daughter will tell you.

Anyway, shortly after this child was born my cousin got a weird fear: She began to worry, for no apparent reason, that her child was going to get leukemia. It's hard to explain how irrational fears come into being—that's why they're irrational. Every time this child got a black-and-blue mark, her mother was convinced that this was the leukemia finally showing a symptom. And she'd take the kid to the pediatrician for a blood test. It actually got to the point where the doctor refused to do any more tests on the girl.

But maybe my cousin had seen *Love Story* too many times. Because she remained convinced that her daughter had leukemia. Every time that little girl fell and got a bruise, it was leukemia. Every time the kid was tired, it was leukemia. It was only a matter of time, my cousin was sure, before a doctor confirmed the horrible truth.

I got sick of hearing "leukemia."

Now, I could have said what any normal person would have said, something along the lines of, "Look, we both know there's nothing really wrong with your daughter, and you've just allowed your imagination to get away from you, so stop being silly, of course she doesn't have leukemia, and everything will be fine." Which, to somebody who's just conjured up a fatal disease for her own flesh and blood, is not going to be even slightly convincing, take it from me.

Telling somebody who's imagining something that they're imagining something is maybe the biggest waste of breath there is.

"Why don't you make it something worse?" I asked my cousin.

"What could be worse?" she said.

"Why don't you picture her entire body covered with big, painful, black-and-blue bruises?" I suggested with a big smile.

"Why would I do such a thing?"

"Why don't you picture her entire body covered with the most hideous bruises you've ever seen? Just make her solid black and blue from head to toe. Because you've already invented this poor child's illness out of nothing. You've already given her a fatal disease. So make it a good one. Try and picture her covered in bruises, wasting away, in a coma, in a hospital bed, in the intensive care unit, with tubes running in and out of her arms and her nose and her mouth. And her stomach."

"That's terrible," my cousin said.

"Good," I told her. "Try and picture it."

She actually did stand there a minute and attempt to imagine her daughter like something out of a bad soap opera, a little child on death's doorstep. At first she scared herself. And then she started to laugh.

"I hate you," she said.

"Thank you," I said.

Now, was she laughing at leukemia? No—she was laughing at herself, at how she had invented a horrible disease for a kid who was in reality healthy as a horse. But she had to take a terrible anxiety and blow it up into the most tragic thing imaginable before she saw how silly she was being. She had to do a little mental judo on herself. And it worked.

At my Canyon Ranch workshops I put people through this all the time. I tell them they have to learn the important skill of catastrophizing.

Here's a good recent example. At the start of the workshop I ask everyone to introduce themselves and say a few words about what's been happening lately. A young woman stood up, told us her name, and said she was sad because just a year or so after her mother died, her father had already remarried. It was too soon, she said, and it made her wonder about how much her father had loved her mother.

"Okay," I told her, "let's start by calling this woman he married The Whore."

That got her attention.

"The Whore looks like a cheap, lowdown Sunset Boulevard streetwalker," I said.

"No, no," the woman said, laughing a little. "She is actually a very elegant lady."

"Oh no she isn't," I said. "We're gonna take her right out of her Chanel suits. She now wears tight miniskirts and fishnet stockings and blouses cut down to here. She's a no-good tramp and she looks like one."

"Now," I said to everybody else in the room, "we're going to create a little story here. Her father married The Whore while he was still grieving over his late wife. And now The Whore is going to steal all this poor man's money."

Everybody laughed.

"She's going to take every nickel that he had planned to leave to his children and grandchildren."

We were all smiling at the story—even the daughter. So I pushed it a little more.

"Not only that, but she's probably going to poison the man with arsenic just so she can get her hands on the money as soon as possible."

At this point the woman really began laughing. We had painted such an ugly, lowdown picture of her father's new wife that she cracked up.

"Okay," I said to her. "I'm glad you're laughing. Now we know what's not real. So let's try and figure out what *is.*"

"I think he just got married too soon," she blurted.

"Too soon for who?"

"For me, I guess."

And before long it was clear that this woman hadn't really allowed herself to feel all the pain inside her as a result of her mother's death. She had come up with the thought that she was pained by her father's remarriage, when that really had little to do with the sadness she was feeling. She would have spent the next year feeling angry at her father and sad about herself. Instead, through creative catastrophizing, she discovered what was really wrong, saw it through from start to finish, and then went on her way. Not exactly ecstatic, but certainly better off than she had been.

8 Issue? I Hardly Know You!

Once upon a time, when you talked about issues you were talking about magazines. Now it means something else. Problems? I guess that's close enough. "He has intimacy issues," you'll hear someone say, meaning that the poor guy they're tearing apart can't get close to people (and no wonder!). Or, "She has food issues," meaning she can't stop putting it in her mouth. The word used to belong to shrinks. It's just one of the many *gifts* they've given us. Nowadays, everybody has issues.

It's such a common term these days that a friend of mine can say, only half-joking, "I have an *ish,*" and everybody knows exactly what he means.

I was in a restaurant and asked for a salad without the mushrooms.

"Don't worry," the waitress said, "I can't stand mushrooms either."

"No kidding," I said.

"I have texture issues," she said, grinning brightly.

It struck me as funny because that's exactly why *I* don't

like mushrooms. It has nothing to do with the taste. I don't like the sponginess.

"I don't eat scallops for the same reason," the waitress said.

"Me either," I replied, and with that we exhausted the subject of our texture issues and could get on with the rest of our lives.

The only good thing about the word is that it allows us to state our weirdnesses loud and clear, without the fear of judgment. If everybody has issues, and we all feel free to discuss them with strangers at the drop of a mushroom cap, then we all accept ourselves a little more easily. We're all a little weird. It feels good to get your weirdness out in the open. We've all got our share.

For instance, I have major teeth issues. You can't imagine.

My teeth are my most treasured possessions and important body part. Breasts, I could care less. They can drop to my kneecaps and I won't notice. I found a lump in my breast once, and of course then the big fear is cancer. But for me, going through the whole process of X ray, surgery, biopsy, waiting for results, was a piece of cake. Not a whimper or a worry. I was sure I didn't have cancer, but even if I did, I wasn't going to fall apart over it. Beyond my control, I reasoned, and worried about other things.

But let me hear that a tooth is in trouble and I go to pieces. I react as though I just heard I'll need a leg amputated.

"My God!" I beg the dentist. "Are you *sure* you can't save it?"

If the answer is no I'll submit, but I refuse to go even one minute with a missing tooth.

"Don't worry," my dentist tells me. "We'll pull the tooth

and then I'll put a bridge in there immediately. You'll never have to see an empty space."

That calms me a little. My dentist, Dr. Saul Pressner, is one of the most important people in my life. I call him my enabler. He knows how absolutely crazed I am about my teeth, and he caters to my insanity. Most people get their teeth cleaned once or twice a year. I go four times, minimum. If I'm feeling anxious about my teeth, I'll go once a month. And I won't let the hygienist near my mouth. Saul cleans my teeth.

In fact, as far as I'm concerned, the nicest thing you can do for me is compliment me on my teeth.

Keep in mind, they're all capped. Still, I need to hear it. This may have something to do with the fact that in reality, my mouth is a mess. I've had fourteen root canals. I don't just have bridges in there—I have tunnels, on-ramps, exits and entrances. You've never seen anything like it. It's not dentistry in there, it's architecture.

But my teeth mean a lot to me. You can call me fat, dumb, or lazy and I won't lose my temper, but insult my teeth and I'll bite you. I'll knock out a few of yours.

My teeth are so tied in with my well-being that if I'm worried or anxious about something, I feel it first in my teeth. If I'm getting ready to travel, for example, some-thing I hate to do, I get a little toothache. Some people feel their angst in their bellies. Mine goes directly to my molars. When I get even a twinge of pain in my teeth, my first question is, "Linda, what's making you unhappy?" It's so sick it's hysterical, and I get a lot of mileage out of making fun of my teeth obsession.

But like all issues, it comes with a painful past. When I was a little girl, I shared a bedroom with my mother. There was a nightstand that separated our beds. On the nightstand was a glass. And every night, into the glass would go my mother's dentures. I would fall asleep staring at those teeth. And every morning I would wake up with them staring at me. They represented everything that was bad, ugly, and disgusting to me. It was like a scene from a horror movie that I saw every day of my life.

My mother let herself go. She gave up on her dignity and self-worth, and she stopped trying to live a happy life. Instead of trying to save her teeth, one day she let the dentist pull them all. Every one. He replaced them with the terrifying false teeth that shared my bedroom. She gave up on everything, and the teeth were a symbol of that. Which is why, I firmly believe, my teeth came to mean so much—why they became such an issue. As long as I had beautiful teeth I knew I wasn't in any immediate danger of becoming my mother. But every time a tooth is threatened, my mind goes back to that glass full of choppers.

Is it any wonder I have teeth issues?

Here's another one—I have whispering issues. I hate whispering! Which also grows out of childhood trauma. I have a vivid memory of the day my father was killed, despite the fact that no one told me what had happened. My memory is of a house crowded with grim-faced relatives, all of them looking at eight-year-old me from time to time and shaking their heads sadly. A great many words were being exchanged, in the most dramatic tones imaginable. But everything was being said in whispers. What they thought they were sparing me I can't imagine. Put yourself in my place—I was scared to death by all the activity around me, but most of all by the fact that I wasn't being told a damn thing. I wasn't eight months old, I was eight years, and a smart, sensitive kid. I was fully aware that something horrible had happened to my life. But I couldn't tell what. It was the cruelest torture possible—if I had known the truth I would have been devastated, but that would have given me the chance to accept reality and learn to deal with it. Here I was being denied even that. The whispering was like its own torment.

To this day, it feels that way. If I see somebody whispering something I'm not meant to hear, I lose my temper. I have been known to reprimand whisperers in a loud voice and demand to be told what was said.

That's my whispering issue. Even that one, I'll admit, is kind of funny. Not as amusing as my teeth issue, maybe, but pretty odd.

I have one issue that even I can't completely laugh about. Oh, it's funny, but it's still a very real problem for me.

My money issue. Now, almost everybody will claim to have some form of money issue. Money's a tough one. You can tell a lot about a person by how they relate to money—whether they're miserly, or spendthrift, or generous only with others, or if they're shopaholics, for instance. A lot of your personality comes through in how you handle money, how you feel about it.

At the root of my money issue is one thing: fear. Fear of poverty. Homelessness, even. And the amount of money I have has almost nothing to do with the level of fear and anxiety that I experience. It's the irrationality that makes it an issue. We all worry about money from time to time. Worrying about money can be a good thing—it makes us prudent, if we're smart. It's what leads us to put some aside for a rainy day.

But my money issues have nothing to do with reality. That's why they're issues.

Again, you don't have to be Sherlock Holmes to figure out why I'm so weird with money. You can start with my childhood.

Part of the reason we were always borderline poor was that my father was dead and my mother was emotionally impaired, meaning she spent a lot of her life functioning at less than full speed ahead. She worked selling coats for commission only, and never earned much. I realized early on that we depended on my aunt and uncle to help us pay the rent. Even as a child I knew there was something odd about that arrangement. I had less than lots of the kids I knew in school, but that didn't really matter much to me. Unlike the kids of today, we were blissfully unaware of the nuances of economics and status back then.

My mother had her own weirdness where money was concerned. One way it came out was in her attitude toward gifts she gave me.

For instance, as a kid I longed to own a tape recorder. I loved to sing—even though I couldn't carry a tune in a dump truck—and wished I could tape songs off the radio so I could hear them whenever I wanted.

So my mother bought me one, a little reel-to-reel job. I loved it, until one day I came home from school, went to the closet to get it, and saw it was gone.

"Ma, where's my tape recorder?" I asked.

"Oh," she said, "I took it back to the store."

"Why?" I cried.

"Because you hardly ever used it. And it was very expensive."

And that was that. I was crushed.

A few years later I craved a typewriter. Again, she came through for me—as a junior high graduation gift, she gave me a Royal.

Three days later, vanished.

"Ma, where's my typewriter?" I asked.

"Returned it," she said.

"But Ma, why?" I wailed.

"Because the novelty already wore off," she said. "You weren't using it."

Now, how conflicted was *she* on the subject of money? You can just picture her, in a fit of love and generosity, buying me the gifts. Then, seized by some demons, she spirited my treasures back to where they came from, knowing exactly how I would react once I discovered the loss. Sick.

Once I got married, of course, I thought I'd be on easy street. My husband was a lawyer, after all, which was supposed to be a one-way ticket to the good life. But he was a lawyer with a crushing gambling addiction, I learned too late. It was just what you'd expect—bills coming in marked "Third Notice," "Final Notice," and then staring at the ringing phone, too afraid to take another call from a collection agency. None of which did anything to relieve my fear of poverty and financial ruin. Meanwhile, my older sister's husband had a red-hot career in advertising, which meant that before long I was dependent on her when the financial situation at home got so tight I was strangling. In other words, I had become my mother—an adult who had to rely on family members for the occasional handout. A fate far worse than death, at least as far as I was concerned.

Then, of course, when the roof came in on us—once my husband's gambling had cost us our home, our car, and all our possessions, once he was forced into bankruptcy—I damn near did become homeless. Just as I always knew I would. In fact, I was homeless once I left him. Sure, I had a roof over my head. I never actually slept in the street. But only because of the generosity of my daughter and son-in-law and other relatives, on whose sofas I spent my nights.

What I'd do back then is parcel myself out, a little at a time. I'd drop in on Robin and Mike, for instance, but I'd only stay for three days. Then I'd pack my bag and move in with my son Jordan for a couple days. Then my sister Judy. My cousin Barbara. Nobody had to endure me for longer than Ben Franklin advised—you know his famous saying: "After three days, fish and house guests begin to stink." I was on steady rotation from couch to couch back then while I tried to get my life in order. Keep in mind, I was a woman in my forties, not exactly a kid. You want to talk about humiliation? Just writing about it makes my cheeks hot (and it ain't menopause).

My career situation at the time did nothing to inspire great financial confidence, I should point out. I had been working as the assistant to a woman who owned a casting company specializing in commercials. I bravely quit my job there and set out on my own, trying to get a foothold in the same business. Of course I had absolutely no money to get my little enterprise off the ground. So it was a scramble both at home (because I was homeless) and at the office (because I was officeless too).

I couldn't afford an office, or even a desk in somebody else's digs. But there was (and still is) a famous skyscraper on Third Avenue, and in the lobby back then was a long bank of phone booths. That became my office. I'd show up every morning at nine o'clock, just like all the other workers. Except instead of boarding an elevator, I'd settle into a phone booth and dig my address book and a roll of quarters out of my portable desk—a Bloomingdale's shopping bag. And I'd begin calling around to the city's ad agencies, trying to drum up work as a casting agent. Thank God it was before the advent of voice mail, so that if the person I was calling wasn't in, I got bounced back to a receptionist, who would then direct my call to the next person on my list.

The restrooms were in the lobby, and they were clean, good thing. I was such a sad sack, the guy who ran the little concession stand near the phones used to give me a candy bar or two every day, just to keep my strength and my spirits up. He could tell I was just barely hanging on. Today they'd probably call the cops on me, but those were gentler times.

At one point, my sister Judy saw how shaky I was, and she urged me strongly to give up on entrepreneurship and get a real nine-to-five job. Something that would give me a steady paycheck and some benefits. I was broke, as usual, and had been depending on her for money to live, which was why I didn't feel I was in a position to ignore her good counsel.

So I did it—I had always been good at selling, so I took a job with an employment agency. It was an adjustment, going from my own loosey-goosey freelance life to being an office drone, but I gave it my all. Starting time there was nine o'clock, but because I'm a morning person I'd be at my desk by eight. And I never stopped for lunch.

Then, on my second day, I rose from my desk at 5:25 P.M., put on my coat, and made for the door.

"Excuse me," the manager said. She was a snippy thing maybe twenty years younger than I was.

"Yes?" I said.

"Where are you going?" she asked.

"Well," I said, "if I hurry, I can make the express bus to Forest Hills—"

"We work until 5:30 here," she interrupted me.

"I know," I said, "but I've been getting in at eight instead of nine, and I didn't stop for lun—"

"We work until 5:30 here," she repeated.

"Hmm," I said. I took a deep breath. Then I said it. What I said was:

"Go fuck yourself." And I walked out the door.

Did that feel great? Oh, no, just the opposite. All the way home I berated myself. "How could you do such a thing?" I asked out loud. "You're going to starve now for sure."

Amazingly, there was some good news waiting for me at home. I had landed my first major casting assignment, one that was way over my head, at least if my experience was any guide. I gave it my all, and, driven by anxiety, I hit a home run on that job. Fear was the fuel, and it propelled me into solvency and even success, eventually.

Which, if I were sane when it came to money, would mean that my nightmare of homelessness and destitution would evaporate. That was not the case, of course. My money issue has no connection to reality. If you're afraid of becoming homeless because you are, in fact, about to become homeless, that's not an issue—that's just a firm grip on reality. An issue is a voyage into unreality.

Here's another example. My business began to really take off during the most woo-woo stage of my spiritual journey following my son's death. This was the time when I was desperate to find the guru, the New Age belief, the strange and wonderful set of rituals that would bring me peace. This was also the time when I developed a serious dependency—on incense.

Now, the incense was perfectly packaged for a looney tunes like me. So there was love incense. Health incense. And prosperity incense. I used to buy prosperity incense by the gross. A few sticks hardly lasted, because I burned it twenty-four hours a day, seven days a week. There were always a fat fistful of prosperity incense sticks smoldering somewhere in my apartment, which served double duty as my office. I was sure that if I burned enough of it, riches would soon be mine. I burned so much of it that my neighbors actually began sending letters of complaint to the building manager's office—they couldn't escape the cloud of prosperity smoke that hung in the halls and clung to the carpets.

Screw 'em, I figured. I had to smell their pot roast. They could put up with my prosperity.

And sure enough, the incense worked! The longer I burned it, the better my business did. Like magic. Only much later did it occur to me that during that period I routinely worked twelve- and fourteen-hour days. In my grief, work was the only thing that could distract me. I never connected the fact that I was a total workaholic with my business's success though—I gave all the credit to the incense. It was almost as though I didn't want to take the credit, because I still didn't believe that I was capable of avoiding poverty on my own efforts.

I also lived well below my means then, as a result of my money issue. This is not necessarily a bad thing, I realize, and a great many people suffer because they have the opposite affliction. The compulsion to spend even what you don't have is also a money issue, and one I'll never have, thankfully. The stress would kill me. I was so bad that I was pulling down a healthy six-figure profit from my business and living in a $700-a-month apartment. But I had also turned into the kind of boss who would underpay people if I could get away with it. Instead of viewing an employee's salary as part of the cost of doing business, I would feel as though it was being taken directly out of my pocket—as though their gain was my loss.

I rewarded people less than their due, and then I'd realize it and feel guilty, so I'd overpay them on their next raise. Or I'd give them a big bonus. Which would only aggravate my money anxieties and cause me to go cheap on the next negotiation. It was a vicious cycle.

Or I'd go to the store and buy some clothes. On the way home, invariably, I'd start to cross-examine myself: Do you really need that suit? Did you have to buy three pairs of shoes? Couldn't you have settled for something a little less pricey? Not that I was spending a lot on clothing, mind you, or going shopping very often. But every time I spent, that voice spoke to me. By the time I got home I was in such a state that more often than not I'd leave the clothes in the bag, knowing that the next day I'd take them back. Crazy.

Or I decided to give up my cheap apartment in Queens and finally buy a place in Manhattan, where all my work existed. I found a perfect place on the Upper East Side, with a terrace and a view of the East River. At last I'd have a little stability and comfort, which would make me feel settled and secure.

Exactly wrong. For the year that I lived there, that apartment gave me nightmares. I wouldn't be able to pay my mortgage. I'd fall behind. Then, before you knew it, I'd lose the place—I'd be homeless again. It was killing me. I knew I could depend on my sister, or my daughter and son-in-law, if I ever had to, but that was as bad as the shame of homelessness itself. It would mean that I had really grown up to become my mother, sponging off of relatives because I was for some reason incapable of taking care of myself. So even thinking about my safety net filled me with shame.

The apartment angst took care of itself, as things almost always do if you are patient and you believe. I was living there and weighing a big, life-changing choice: Did I really want to move to Tucson to work full-time at Canyon Ranch? I couldn't decide. I was up and down. I'd decide to go, then I'd change my mind.

One night at about ten o'clock I was pondering that very question when the doorman called to ask if mine was the apartment listed for sale, because Dr. So-and-so, who lived in the building, was looking to buy another unit. Being a great believer in serendipity, and not worrying that I might be diverting a buyer from the apartment that actually was for sale, I said yes. A moment passed and the doctor was on the phone, asking if he could come up and see the place.

"Sure thing," I said.

"It's 7-C, right?" he asked.

"No, 9-C," I corrected him.

Fifteen minutes later the good doctor was at my door. I happily conducted the grand tour, and when it was through he made me an offer that was about twice what I had paid a year before. I accepted, we shook hands, and then I started packing a few boxes of my possessions. Soon I retired to sleep the sleep of the just and the pure. Deep, dreamless, and totally lacking in any of the anxiety that had been a part of my life for some time. First, I was unloading this apartment that had filled me with such dread. And second, since I was moving out, I was obviously moving to Tucson.

Another manifestation of my money issue is that I cannot stand to receive a bill. I don't care how small it is—just the thought of it makes my stomach clench. As I've said, a lot of these reactions were acquired during my marriage, when I had ample reason to die inside every time the mailman delivered or the phone rang. But I was already disposed to money anxiety, so the marriage only brought it to full flower.

When I first went to my dentist, Saul, I had no money and no insurance. He examined me and determined that I needed a bit of work—oh, maybe $10,000 worth.

"Saul, I can't pay," I said.

"Don't worry," he said. "We'll do the work now and you'll pay me when you can."

"But Saul," I said, "you have to promise never to send

me a bill. I'll gladly pay you for the work. But if I ever see a bill for $10,000, I'll drop dead. I mean it."

"Don't worry," he said. He really is the Prince of Dentistry. "You'll never get a bill. You just pay when you can."

"And what if I can *never* pay?" I asked.

"Then you'll never pay," he said.

I did pay, over time. But I never knew what I owed. I just sent money when I had it until he told me to stop.

Even now, all my bills go to my bookkeeper in New York. I never write a check. She knows how much money should be in my account, and if it gets low she tells me how much dough to shift over to her. Once she said, "Linda, you spent a lot on clothes last month." I almost bit her head off. I mean I really lost my temper. I never want to hear that, I said. It was partly because what I spend is my business, and I don't want to have to answer for it. But more than that, even, was that hearing I had spent money on clothes gave me a nasty chill down my spine.

When the account she controls is in need of money, she very gingerly tells me so. I then say, as swiftly as I can, "Fine, you know what to do, just please take care of it right away." I can't even bear to hold the conversation.

All my various investments and assets are watched over by my financial planner, who keeps up with the details so I don't have to. I control the money, of course, and not too much mayhem could take place without me knowing. But I refuse to know the details. It's not that—I can't bear to know. Every month I call him and ask, "Okay, how much am I worth?" And he tells me the exact number. If it's larger than the month before, I breathe a huge sigh of relief and go on with my life in blissful ignorance. Because if it's not larger than the month before, I am plunged back into despair and anxiety.

Here's how bad it gets—sometimes I end up so panicked

over money that I have to call my therapist, Dr. Dan Baker, whom I first met at Canyon Ranch. Together, he and I have dealt with a lot of the problems and neuroses that beset my life. But this money one is stubborn. So I still make the calls from time to time.

"All right, let's slow down a little," he'll say. "Stop thinking and answer a few questions for me."

"Okay," I'll say.

"Do you have enough money in the bank to pay this month's mortgage?"

"Yes," I'll reply.

"No," he says. "I want you to say it in a sentence."

"I have enough money to make this month's mortgage payment," I dutifully say.

"Okay," he says, "how about the phone bill?"

"I can pay this month's phone bill."

"Can you buy food?"

"I can buy food."

"Can you pay your utilities?"

"I can pay my utilities."

"If you wanted to go out to dinner, can you afford to go?"

"I can afford to go out to dinner . . ."

We go on that way for a while.

Once we've covered all the essentials, I begin to relax. He directs me to break my finances down into the smallest possible compartments, so I can see that there's no great big disaster about to overwhelm me.

The funniest part of all this, of course, is that for those phone sessions Dr. Dan charges his usual rate—$165 an hour. So my money issues ease my mind even as they drain my bank account.

We both laugh over that, him a little harder than me.

In the end though, I am able to use my own techniques

to ease my mind most of the time. Because my greatest fear is that I'll end up homeless, I try to imagine exactly what that will be like. I picture myself not just mooching off my family—in my imagination, I'm sleeping in an empty refrigerator box on a street somewhere in Manhattan. It's cold and damp and all I have are the clothes on my back. I'm broke, so of course I can't even feed myself, and there I am rummaging through trash cans and Dumpsters for old pizza crusts and Chinese food containers.

I am the picture of a shopping bag lady, except that I'm wearing my Donna Karan shoes. That's all I own in the way of footwear, and so of course if I were suddenly out on the street that's what I'd have on. I picture this middle-aged woman sleeping out in the elements, on a vent or the steps of a church, filthy, bedraggled, a wretch—wearing pink Donna Karan mules. And then I laugh.

But only until the next time my money issues raise their scary head. This book is supposed to help people, but I'm sorry to say that on the subject of incurable issues I am no help at all. Unless it's news to you that we're all highly imperfect. I once read that in Turkistan (or someplace over there), the rug-weavers always intentionally include one flaw, because only God is perfect. Sounds sensible to me— I don't want to be *too* perfect.

9 A Tale of Two Sammys

I don't want you to think it's just *my* stories that are so fascinating and filled with life lessons—my friends' stories are fascinating and filled with life lessons too! And none more so than the story of Happy Sammy and Sad Sammy.

I lived next door to Sad Sammy in Queens for more than ten years, so I knew him pretty well, but believe me, anyone could see he was an unhappy man. You could read the misery all over his face. He worked hard for forty-some years at a major publishing company in New York. He wasn't some workaholic top executive or a powerhouse salesman, though—he slaved all those years in the customer service department. So he never made a ton of money. But he supported a wife and kids and a house and all the rest. It was a hard, boring, stressful, thankless job, but he dragged himself to it every day. Then, every night, he dragged himself home, ate his dinner, and went off to enjoy his favorite pastime: fish. He would pour himself a big glass of scotch and sit by himself in a room and stare at his fish tank. That was his joy—watching tropical fish swim circles in a glass box. Even they were having more fun than he was.

I can sum up Sad Sammy's outlook on life in one exchange we had just before he retired.

"Sammy," I said, "if you hated it so much, why did you stay so long?"

"The benefits!" he said.

The benefits? What was the benefit of spending your entire life doing something you hated? Who benefits from that?

Happy Sammy I've known even longer. Until he retired, he also worked hard at a job that never made him rich, as a salesman in the printing business. But he was one of those guys who just radiates happiness. He knew everybody, and everybody knew him. He was always on the go, and you smiled just to see him, because in addition to being full of good cheer, he was also an extremely good-looking guy. When he got home from work, he didn't stare at his guppies—he immediately took a quick nap so he'd have energy for later, when he went out to the movies, or to play cards, or dancing. Weekend days he was on the greens, because he loved golfing too.

To Sad Sammy, life was toil and hardship and responsibility. He thought that grown-ups had to be drudges, and so he played the part without a complaint. As he understood it, life wasn't supposed to be fun. You work hard and pay your mortgage and your taxes and keep a roof over everybody's head and that's reality. His wife, by the way, was exactly the same. They saw life in the same way and reinforced each other's misery.

Happy Sammy, of course, had somehow gotten the idea that life was meant for his enjoyment, and so he lived it that way. You could even say that Happy Sammy went a little overboard in that direction—he was having an awful lot of fun. Maybe he even neglected some of his domestic duties. But if you're going to go overboard in one direction or the other, he made the right choice, I think.

Obviously, their approaches to life grew out of how they thought it was meant to be. But how did the two Sammys get such different expectations? Well, that's an easy one—their mothers were as different as they are.

Happy Sammy's mother was even bouncier than her son. There was lots of singing and dancing and playing in that house. Lots of joy. Things were maybe a little too carefree and footloose and happy-go-lucky around Happy Sammy's home. But better too much joy than not enough. That's what he was used to—that's the way he thought life was supposed to be.

Sad Sammy's mother was one of those old immigrants who goes through life expecting the worst. To her, famine, calamity, and poverty were always right around the corner. Fun was for three-year-olds. To make matters even worse, she was a concentration camp survivor. A woman who had gone through unimaginable anguish. So the nightmare was always close at hand. That household was all gloom and doom. Now, could you blame her? No. Just as you couldn't give Happy Sammy's mother the credit for having such a sunny outlook on life. They had both been formed by *their* mothers and *their* experiences. And on and on it goes. In the mother sweepstakes, Happy Sammy got lucky and Sad Sammy did not.

Now, of course, life isn't one hundred percent balloons and birthday cakes for anybody, and one day Happy Sammy lost his smile. He got physically sick and required surgery. Nothing life-threatening, but then there were postsurgery complications. It was the first time he had ever been ill, and it actually threw him into a depression.

Happy Sammy in a depression was quite an unusual

thing, as you can imagine. In his mind, it was red alert—time for emergency measures. Imagine if tomorrow you woke up and it felt like your foot was about to fall off. You'd worry. That's how depression felt to Happy Sammy.

So he did the most sensible thing possible—he asked for help. He didn't go a week in that condition. He found a therapist, and he and the doctor spent a couple months talking. After that, Happy Sammy felt happy again. No more therapist. No more depression.

Sad Sammy had been depressed all his life. Here's a guy who probably would have benefited a great deal from therapy. But he never went. He never even knew he was depressed. Because if you've always been depressed, you have no way of knowing it! Depression just feels normal to you. You go through life thinking that's how everybody feels. You think that's how you're supposed to feel.

That was Sad Sammy. So sad he didn't even know it.

The one big thing Happy Sammy and Sad Sammy had in common was this: They both clung to what they were used to. Happy Sammy was used to being happy. He had been happy his whole life. His mother before him had been happy too. So for him, happy was the way things are supposed to be. He's a lucky guy. Not everybody goes through life feeling that way. And when, for a moment, he felt sad, he realized something was terribly wrong, and he got it fixed right away.

Sad Sammy was used to being sad. He had been sad his whole life. His mother before him had been sad. So for him, sad was the way you're supposed to be. He was an unlucky guy, you could say.

The lesson I took from the two Sammys was that if you look at your life and you can honestly say that you're accustomed to happiness and pleasure and joy, you're in good shape. You won the Lotto. But if you look back and see that you grew up accustomed to unhappiness and misery and angst and depression, you've got to be on guard. Because we all feel most comfortable with what we're accustomed to. If, like Sad Sammy, you have lived accustomed to sadness, you may not even know how sad you are. You may not know all the joy you're missing that's easily within your grasp. You may not know there's a way out. It's hard to choose the way you're *not* accustomed to. But the sad ones have to do just that. They have to struggle against what feels most comfortable. Or they'll be sad ones forever.

Now then, some people may take all this to mean that happiness or sadness are predestined and beyond our control—that it all comes down to who your mother was, and that's that. Which is *not* at all what I'm saying. Sad Sammy *could* have lived a much happier life. He even might have felt joy once or twice. But he never seized the reins—he never took action on his own behalf to *make* himself happy. He allowed his life to just *happen* to him. Which is the exact opposite of Happy Sammy's good example.

And by the way, there's a capper to the tale of two Sammys. Guess what Sad Sammy's going to be doing with his benefits? Well, he just found out he has leukemia! Could you hang yourself? Could it be any worse? He put off having fun until after he retired, and this is how he'll spend his golden years. He's going to make good use of those benefits, that's for sure. He'll have top medical care, and his wife will live off a great pension.

Now, did living a miserable life give Sad Sammy this terrible disease? No, I don't believe so. But if you're going to get leukemia someday no matter *what* you do, shouldn't you have as much fun as possible right now?

10 Try It, It Works for Me: Waving the Red Flag

If you take one lesson from the two Sammys, let it be this: It pays to pay attention to your mental state. Happy Sammy noticed it the second he began feeling depressed, and he did something about it right away. Sad Sammy had been sad for so long that he couldn't tell the difference. For him, sad was a way of life, and he never even tried to get himself happy.

I pay a great deal of attention to my inner state. You could say I'm in a constant conversation with myself that I interrupt only for sleep and other important diversions. Maybe it sounds a little self-involved, but guess what? Better to pay too much attention to your well-being than not enough. When I am in the slightest danger of falling into a depression or some other harmful state, I want to know about it in advance so I can head it off. If I never see it coming, I'll never know to defend myself.

So I go through life looking for my "red flags"—the signs of impending trouble. Everybody's warning signals are different, but we all have them. The important thing is to identify yours and then get vigilant, so the second a problem rears its ugly little head, you see it and give it a good hard smack.

Here's a red flag of mine that's almost universal—some days I have a little trouble getting out of bed. It happens to us all. I'm not talking about flat-on-your-back, pinned-to-the-mattress, paralyzing depression. Just maybe you're half a step slower than usual getting up and out. You're slightly sluggish. It's such a subtle thing that maybe you don't even feel it.

But there's something going on, and it's throwing a gray cloud over our usual zest for life. Maybe it's something at work, or at school. It could be a marriage thing or a kid thing. Whatever it is, we dread it, and we dread thinking about it, and the only place we feel safe is in bed, preferably sound asleep. Nothing (except our own dreams, of course) can get us when we sleep. No wonder that's where I hold all my pity parties. I live alone, so it's not as though I need to stay in my bed to avoid human contact. But bed is safe. Bed is like the womb, only drier and with better TV reception. So the reluctance to leave bed (except with certain obvious exceptions) is a good warning of trouble out there somewhere.

When I'm a little slow getting up, I put everything aside for a few minutes and ask myself some important questions: What's going on in my life right now? What could be making me a little anxious? Is there something coming up today that I don't want to face? Is there a phone call I have to make, or a meeting, or maybe an appointment of some kind? Do I have to see the doctor, for instance? Is there some unpleasant news I'm anticipating? Or is it just that life has become depressing in an overall, nonspecific way?

Sometimes even *I* have a little trouble figuring it out.

"Linda," I say, "is something wrong?"

"No, not a thing," I say.

"Are you sure?" I ask.

"Yes, I'm sure, everything's fine," I insist.

"Will you please think about it a minute before you answer?"

"Listen, I'm thinking and everything is okay, okay?"

"Come on, there's something," I say.

"What?" I reply.

"How the hell do I know?" I say. "*You* figure it out."

In the end I usually win the argument—there *is* something that's preying on my mind and clouding my mood. Whenever you feel lousy, there's always a reason. People are tempted to take the easy way out and just shrug and go on as though everything's normal. That's a mistake. In the long run you save time and anguish if you deal with problems the second you notice them.

Because I am a very practical-minded person, I like to take lessons from the most nuts-and-bolts things imaginable. For example, I learned to deal with these red flag warnings partly by learning to deal with car trouble.

I start the car one morning and hear a weird new noise. Like, a "hrrrr, hrrrr . . ." Two seconds of that and my anxieties begin to kick in. I am the least mechanical person in the world. I have no idea what makes my car run or what stops it dead. All I know is that noise doesn't belong.

And so the worrying begins. What's making that terrible sound? Is it something serious or not? Can I drive around like this forever or will the car die as soon as I get out on one of those lonesome desert roads? How long before the brakes fail or the engine falls out or the transmission explodes or whatever is about to go wrong? You can drive and drive and listen to that "hrrr, hrrr . . ." and all you do is wait and worry and worry and wait.

The noise refuses to go away, and your nerves finally get the better of you and you start thinking about all those rattlesnakes that live in the desert just waiting for somebody's car to break down, until you finally wise up and take the car to the mechanic and make it his problem. You've done all you can. You can relax now (until you get the bill).

Today I don't even wait that long. Now I start the car, I hear the "hrrr, hrrr . . ." and I drive immediately to the mechanic. I don't even call him first. Because I know that the noise is going to drive me insane with worry, and that's not going to do me any good, and it won't help the car a bit either.

If it makes sense for a car, it usually makes sense for a person too.

To say, "I just feel a little down," is meaningless—you feel it for a reason. And if you don't deal with it when it's little, you may be allowing it to grow big. You take it to the mechanic right away. And the mechanic is you. (Or your shrink.)

I'll tell you another big red flag in my life—agoraphobia. The inability to leave the house for eleven years definitely qualifies as a sign that something's maybe a tiny bit wrong, wouldn't you say? Maybe after even two or three years you'd say to yourself, "This just isn't right!" Well, it took me a while.

Actually, there were red flags that came before the agoraphobia, warning signals I should have paid attention to at once. These were the panic attacks—I'd suddenly get short of breath, like something was squeezing my lungs shut. I'd sweat. I'd get dizzier than I've ever been in my life. My hands grew numb. All physical symptoms. They lasted for twenty minutes, tops, then went away. If you suddenly got one, you'd think you were having a heart attack, or some kind of lung disorder. That's how it feels.

In fact, I went right away to my doctor, who sent me to a neurologist, who ran all the brain wave tests and everything else they had back then. Not a clue as to what might be wrong.

Finally the doctor had to make some kind of pronouncement.

"We think it's nerves," he said gravely.

I still love that word. Back then, if it was a problem inside a woman's head and they couldn't figure out why, it was *nerves*. Guaranteed.

I can't blame the doctors though. There was no clue as to what might be wrong with me. Except, of course, that the attacks came only when I was away from home. Imagine how eager you'd be to leave the house if every time you did you had a heart attack. You'd become a shut-in too.

The agoraphobia was just a response to the panic attacks. Had I known then what I know now, I would have asked myself after the first panic attack, "Linda, what's wrong in your life?"

If I had had the insight to answer that question—which at the time I did not, believe me—I would have answered something like this:

"Linda, it's just the buildup, over time, of so many emotional problems and shocks that I've never properly dealt with. From the unexplained death of my father, which was never even spoken of in my presence, to the chronic mental illness of my mother and then the death of my aunt, who had been the only real stable adult force in my life, I allowed all that stuff to go unresolved, unabsorbed, which is why at this particular moment it feels like somebody is standing on my chest and somebody else is kneeling on my windpipe and I'm sweating and feeling more anxious and fearful than I've ever felt in my entire life."

That's what I would have said.

And if I had been able to say such a thing, I never would have had the agoraphobia, because I'd be managing my problems instead of letting them manage me.

Here's another of my red flags that lots of people share. I suddenly begin to overreact to the normal minor irritations of life. Somebody says something you'd normally laugh at, or shrug off. This time you fly off the handle. You erupt in anger. Or you seethe in silence. Either way, you're good and pissed. Whenever that happens, I ask myself, "Why?" If I have a perfectly good reason for being angry, then I'm fine. I have no problem getting mad when the occasion calls for it.

But once in a while, even *I* know that my reaction is out of proportion to what's just been said or done to me.

Somebody will say, "Oh, Linda, is your hair different?"

To which I might normally reply, "No, why do you ask?"

But then, once in a while, such a question might cause me to think:

"What's wrong with my hair, you ugly, insulting bitch!"

On those days, I allow for the fact that something might be bothering me. And so the self-interview begins, and goes on until I get to the bottom of things.

Feeling sick is a red flag that we should all recognize. Sometimes—maybe most of the time—a physical ailment is purely physical. An upset stomach. A bad back. Aches and pains. But there are times when the source of these pains is psychological or emotional. By now only the most stubborn old-fashioned thinkers refuse to see the connection between mind and body. You can easily make yourself sick with worry or stress. So every time I feel sick I first ask myself, "Linda, is this from something that's bothering you?" I can't always figure it out so easily, but I always try. Sometimes, if I can get at the source of my anxiety, the ache or pain magically goes away.

I don't suffer from back pain, but I know people who do. More than one of them has reported that after trying medicine, surgery, exercise, chiropractic, all to no avail, they have been helped by Dr. John Sarno. His books are all bestsellers, and he insists that most back pain is due to repressed anger or other unhappiness. Let out the bad feelings and deal with them, he says, and almost all back pain vanishes.

Exhaustion is a red flag. When you're tired, you're vulnerable in every way, physical as well as emotional. You're more likely to catch a flu when you're exhausted, so why wouldn't you be more likely to feel depressed too? So I make sure to get my beauty sleep. I am the world's worst flier—I get bored and antsy and taxed. Throw in a few layovers and I'm completely strung out. So when I fly I pack my special carry-on bag. It's my activity bag—I have to pack for myself as though I'm a hyperactive ten-year-old about to take a long car trip. I bring two or three books to read. Highlighters, so I can find important passages later when I need them. Crossword puzzles. Knitting. Anything I can think of to keep me from getting bored. Because bored makes me tired. And tired makes me vulnerable.

And a final red flag for me is chaos—or rather, my reaction *to* chaos. This comes up over and over in my life—the chaos of my childhood, the way my father's death was handled, and my mother's inability to provide a normal, stable life haunt me to this day. Any kind of disorder or confusion drives me insane. Noise kills me. When I return to New York now, the hustle and bustle of the city overwhelms me. I hate crossing the street. I hate going to restaurants. I hate shopping. Any kind of confusion and uncertainty will, I am certain, ruin my day. Once I was trying to arrange for a little vacation with some friends in San Diego. They were arguing back and forth about the hotels and how the cheap ones were far from the water but the ones with a view of the Pacific were too expensive, and maybe they could save a few bucks on the airfare and on and on and around and around until finally I said, "That's it for me! Either we stop this conversation now and just decide to stay on the water, or you can both go alone, because I've had it!"

That brought the conversation to a close in a hurry, let me tell you. I know how rude and high-handed I sounded, but the confusion was killing me. Luckily, these were real friends, so they overlook my red flag moments.

Travels in the Spirit World

Every guru and therapist and social worker and self-help expert I've ever met is nuts. Every one of them—all cuckoo.

Which makes perfect sense. When you help other people with their problems, you feel better about yourself. It makes you figure, "Well, how bad off can I be if I am capable of helping somebody else feel better, or even helping them to change the way they behave?" Why would anybody go into one of the helping fields if not because they've felt in need of help themselves? It all has to add up deep inside you—nobody grows up and says, "Okay, am I gonna be a psychiatrist or an auto mechanic? Am I gonna help people find the path to total spiritual fulfillment, or am I gonna be a TV news anchor?" Mel Zuckerman, the man behind Canyon Ranch, puts it something like this: "The helper who does the most good is drawn from the deepest, darkest shadow."

It's even possible that you have some issues you haven't dealt with, and you find it's easier to deal with them in the lives of other people. Not the most altruistic thought in the world, but we all need personal reasons for doing things, especially for doing things well. We have to get something out of it, some need has to be met, otherwise why would we work and try so hard to make somebody else feel better? These insights have come to me over the course of time, starting back when I first sought the help of a therapist. I know now that there's a thin line between the helper and the helpee—once you've been helped, it can really inspire you to help others. It's amazing how easily you can even go back and forth between those two roles.

I say all this as a way of getting into the subject of my own spiritual journey. Now, I realize how lofty that sounds—"my spiritual journey," as though I'm Gandhi or maybe even Shirley MacLaine, off on some mind-bending mystical voyage of the soul. That's not what I'm talking about. I just mean that once you've admitted that you can't manage your problems alone is when you start to look for something bigger and more powerful you can tap into for help. Doing just that—acknowledging that maybe there *is* something bigger than you, and believing that it can make sense of your life—is, to me, what spirituality is all about. If I could think of another word for it, believe me, I'd use it.

My own journey toward finding a better life starts with a shrink. The first time I realized that I didn't have to remain trapped inside my own misery, it was thanks to a psychiatrist. My spiritual journey will certainly go on until my life ends (or until I attain total perfection of mind and soul, whichever comes first), but the person who has been crucial to my life most recently is also a shrink. Maybe it's just that in previous centuries we believed in religion and looked to holy men, and nowadays we believe in science and look to shrinks. Not much difference there.

I was around twenty when I first sought out help. I had a very nuts-and-bolts reason for doing so. A friend of mine, a woman named Karen, had just had what everyone called "a complete nervous breakdown." I wasn't exactly sure what that meant, and I don't know if anyone else knew either, but it sounded interesting and quite possibly like something I had been experiencing on and off my entire life. The only other person I ever knew who had a nervous breakdown was my mother, and since I was sure that I was going to turn into her someday, I figured it was something I should be on the lookout for anyway.

So when Karen got out of the hospital I called her up. She informed me that her therapist had given her pills and they had made all the difference in the world. That sounded pretty good to me—if somebody could just prescribe me a pill and solve all my anxieties and problems, wonderful. I was and still am the kind of person who hates to take pills of any kind, even aspirin, but if a pill would end my misery I would gladly have taken a whole medicine chest.

So I went to a shrink. Not Karen's shrink, because he was too expensive. Another one, a woman whose name I can still recall these forty years later: Betty Graham.

"Why are you here?" she asked at the start of our first session.

"I don't want to be like my mother, and I don't know how *not* to be," I said.

"Okay," she said.

"Is there a pill you can give me?" I asked.

"A pill?"

I told her all about Karen and the pills her doctor had prescribed.

"We're going to talk instead," she said.

"Talk," I repeated, and meanwhile I'm thinking, *What a waste of time this turned out to be.* Because talking wasn't going to change my life. Maybe a pill wouldn't either, but it made sense to me that if I took one *something* would be different. Maybe I would be different enough to deal with my various burdens and not go permanently insane like you-know-who.

"Let's talk about your mother," she said.

And at that moment, my life began to change. That stands out in my mind even today as the first step on the road from sickness to health. There have been many crucial turning points in my life. But that was the first. As I've said elsewhere, I felt as though up until then I had been caught in a whirlpool, and at that moment I swam my first stroke away from it. The whirlpool, of course, was the fear that I could not escape the terrible influence of my mother—that she would pull me under the waves with her. One nudge from a psychiatrist and suddenly I felt a little shudder of hope that maybe I *could* avoid the fate that most terrified me.

I know how melodramatic that sounds. But it really does feel that way when you're in the thick of it. And there's nothing wrong with a little melodrama here and there—everybody's life should have a few moments like that. It's only when you've got melodrama every twenty minutes that you have to figure something's wrong somewhere.

And it turned out that I *loved* talking with Betty Graham. Every Thursday morning at ten o'clock, she and I sat down together and tried to figure out my life as if it were a puzzle. We were detectives on a case together, chasing down leads like on a cop show, my favorite form of TV entertainment.

All my life people have told me I'm a searcher and a seeker. They don't mean it on any kind of highfalutin level, believe me. But I *am* the kind of person who's always looking for ways to make life better. I want to improve things.

I don't feel threatened or discouraged by admitting there's room for improvement. It's part of my personality. It's not good or bad—it just *is*. And therefore, at every moment of my life when things have gone other than how I want them to go, or I'm feeling other than how I want to feel, I have been the kind of person who sits down and says: *Hmmm. What's wrong here? Why am I unhappy? What can I do that will make me feel better? How can I change the way things happen? How can I change the way I'm thinking about this?* For the forty-some years of my adult life, that impulse has been my constant companion and my saving grace. I hate to think of what a mess I'd be if I weren't this way.

It's a funny thing though, this need to strive, to do better, to improve. One way that comes out in some people is in the quest for more material satisfaction. They find themselves dissatisfied with how much money they have, and so they try hard to make more. It's not even that they *need* more money. It's just that they think more will make them happier.

The biggest lesson I've learned in my time working at Canyon Ranch is that money can't make you happy. Now, that may sound like the oldest chapter in the book, like something your grandmother told you—your slow grandmother—and I'm treating it like some big revelation. But it wasn't until I began working here that that old cliché really sank in. Here, I am in constant contact with the richest of the rich—the men and women who measure their wealth in hundreds of millions, and even more than that. There's not a thing you can think of that they can't buy. And no matter how they spend, they earn it even faster— their daily interest is more than you or I could blow on a dare. Yet so many of these people are among the most miserable souls I know. They still want more. Or they're afraid somebody is trying to cheat them out of what they own.

Or they just hit that empty spot—they always thought that if they had enough money they'd be happy and home free. Now they have the fortune, and lo and behold—still miserable and anxious and gloomy. Still insecure. Still wanting something.

That "wanting" can be a sure sign that somebody's in trouble. I'm thinking of a woman I know back in New York. She has a little business she runs out of her apartment, nothing big or prestigious or lucrative. But it's something she's good at, and she takes pride in her work, and it pays the bills with a little left over. She couldn't have a child of her own, so she adopted a little girl, and she's crazy over the moon with this kid. She has a husband too—he was kind of shaky there for a while, it looked like maybe she had made a bad choice. But she hung in there with him, she didn't give up, she encouraged him all she could, but mostly she was patient and loving and kind. And sure enough he straightened out and got rid of his bad habits and now he's on the good track. He has a steady job, but he's strictly a working joe, a face in the crowd. He has no hope of hitting it big or going public or anything like that. No realistic prospects of luxury in this lifetime.

And that's my friend's life. She is maybe the happiest person I know.

She's not brain-dead, mind you—she's actually pretty bright. She has a temper when things go wrong. But she is absolutely at peace inside her skin. Somehow, this woman knew how to find contentment, and it has nothing to do with money or possessions or prestige or anything like that. If somebody in her family gets sick, she's upset. That's when she wishes things were different. But otherwise, life as it is is good enough for her. She buys a bracelet from QVC and you'd think somebody took her to Tiffany.

Now, if my friends from Canyon Ranch had to live this

woman's life, they'd be out on the ledge taping a good-bye note to the windowsill. If they knew this woman they'd think, "What's wrong with her, how can she settle for so little, how can her horizons be so low?" They'd tell one another, "Well, clearly she has self-esteem problems, or else she'd believe she deserves more blah blah blah . . ." And they'd be completely wrong.

I envy this woman. I even idolize her. Without making any big fuss about it, she is the most spiritual person I know. She doesn't need one thing more than she has. There are women with millions and millions more, and they're the unhappiest creatures on the planet. Unlike them, this girl is content. She has all that she needs inside her, and nobody can take it away. If that's not a state of spiritual well-being, then I don't know what is.

The lesson is clear—if you have to depend on externals to make you happy, then your happiness will never be secure. It will always require conditions over which you may have no control. Whereas if you're able to find contentment from the inside, your happiness is there for good.

This would be a great little lesson if I could tell you how to find the kind of peace and tranquillity and contentment my friend has found. But I can't. Like I said, I wish I had some of what she has. I do have *some*—but not at her level. If I tell her that, she'll laugh, but she won't contradict me. She's not a big spiritual talker. I doubt that she's ever had a conversation with anybody on the subject of spirituality and inner peace and all that jazz. She just lives it. She *is* it. Which is why she doesn't have to talk about it. And that brings me back to where this thought started—that the people who try to help or teach about sanity (me included) are the real nuts and malcontents. But we're trying, at least. Sometimes we're the ones who look or sound the silliest. That's a chance we have to take. There are worse risks.

Up until a very specific point in my life, I thought religion was pure nonsense and utter stupidity. I was not raised in a religious household. My mother, after all, was a little Jewish girl raised in an orphanage run by Catholic nuns. Is that a recipe for a schizo outlook on religion? Where was she going to pick up Judaism? And though in our family we all certainly felt Jewish, and lived among Jews, we were not religious by any stretch of the imagination. Culturally, nobody was more Jewish than me. But in terms of actually going to temple or observing a religion? I had no time for it.

I was perfectly happy going along that way until my son died. That turned me around in a hurry.

My son's death turned me into a crazy lady. I was in agony from the grief. But I recall vividly that even in the depths of my pain and despair, a question arose:

What would Rose Kennedy do?

Because if there ever was an expert on handling the death of a child, let's face it, it was Rose Kennedy. I lost one child? She lost four! Mine was too young to die? So were hers. Mine died suddenly and unexpectedly? How about two assassinations?

Think she felt much pain? Think she had to dig deep to find a reason to live?

Anyway, I am a practical-minded person. So I said to myself, I'm gonna find out what Rose Kennedy did, and I'm gonna do it too. I started going to the library and taking out books on the Kennedys. I read everything ever written about Rose. And the one thing they all said was that she relied on her faith in God to get her through the darkest hours. They said she believed in a power greater than herself, and didn't dwell on whether losing three beautiful young sons and a daughter was unfair or not. She believed and she prevailed.

Okay, I said. If it's good enough for Rose Kennedy, it's good enough for me. God kept her sane and whole, and he or it was going to do the same again. All I had to do was find God wherever she had been hiding throughout my life thus far, and I would be okay.

(A quick digression: Years later I met Maria Shriver, and I couldn't wait to ask her the question I had been carrying around with me. "How did your grandmother do it?" I asked. "You got me," she replied. "I would have crumbled. I really have no idea how she hung in there like that." Ha!)

First I looked for God in a predictable place—a synagogue. One day not long after my son died I was walking in Manhattan, on the Upper East Side, on my way to the dentist's office. Suddenly, the sadness came down on me like a lead weight. I felt that I was about to really lose my grip and become hysterical. That's how it happens when you suffer a loss like that—you're going along minding your own business and all at once it overtakes you and leaves you helpless. Anyway, this was such a moment, and then suddenly I look up and see A Synagogue. Perfect, I thought—it's a sign. God is steering me here. I'll go in and sit quietly for a little while and collect my wits. Who knows what else will come to me while I'm here?

I knocked on the door and a woman answered and I said, "Listen, please, I just need to come in for a few minutes. I'm in the middle of a rough time." As I recall, I was crying as I spoke.

"I'm sorry, we're closed now," she said. "Come back after one o'clock."

"No, you don't understand," I said. "I just lost my son.

I am about to collapse here on the street. I need to sit down someplace quiet *right now.*"

"I see," she said, "but you'll still have to come back. We open at one."

"I need to pray *now!*" I insisted. To be truthful, I had never prayed in my life and had no idea how to do it, but I was going to say anything if it might convince her to cut me a break.

"You'll have to come back later," she said. And with that she closed the door in my sobbing face.

Well, now I was really in trouble. I was weeping like a madwoman, like a two-year-old who lost her mommy, on the streets of Manhattan in the middle of a weekday morning. If you had seen me walking your way, you would have crossed the street.

Then I looked down the block and saw big doors, wide open.

Another sign from God? I looked closer. A Presbyterian church.

Why not? I asked myself. What's the difference where I sit? If the Jews won't take me in, maybe the Presbyterians will.

I was a little worried, I'll admit it. I wondered: Will I get struck by lightning? But when I looked inside I didn't see any big statues of Jesus or the saints or anything like that to scare me off. It was a fairly plain, unadorned interior. So I went in. Still weeping.

"Is there something I can do to help?" I heard a voice say. It was a man, looking a little concerned. I don't know if he was a reverend or a rector or a pastor or what.

"No, nobody can help me," I said.

"Would you like to just sit here?" he asked.

"Is that okay?" I asked.

"Yes," he said. "I'll leave you alone."

I sat there for hours. Doing nothing but crying. People came and went, but nobody bothered me or made me answer any questions. They gave me total privacy in this very public place. I really felt that day that the Presbyterians had saved my life. Whereas the Jews wouldn't even open the door. For a while, as a result of that, I was mad at all the Jews. Now I'm just mad at that bitch who wouldn't let me in.

This isn't my line, but I read it somewhere and I agree: When my son died, I put God on trial and found him guilty. I didn't feel the need for God in my life before that terrible fate befell my baby boy. I wasn't even convinced he existed. But once Jordan died, suddenly I believed in God big time, only I was pissed at him for letting it happen. The same thing happened with the synagogue—I had no need for temple until my world fell apart, and when it did I found fault with all of Judaism.

Anyway, maybe if I had been a good Catholic girl like Rose Kennedy I would have found solace. Maybe if I had been a good Jewish girl I would have found solace. Unfortunately, those two options were pretty much closed off to me.

So I began to make it up as I went.

Because therapy had been such a lifesaver to me before, that's one direction in which I turned. I actually found a therapist who had lost a child in a car accident! I tried my best to stay busy every day too, knowing that too much time to think was going to make things more difficult.

But staying busy was easier said than done. I just lost the capacity to do all the little mindless things we do to get through life. I was suddenly unable to pay any bills, because I had mysteriously lost the ability to write checks! Amazing what you can lose, isn't it? At one point American

Express called and wondered why a steady payer like me had suddenly gone three months without paying a bill.

"My son died," I told the woman on the phone, as though that would be a sensible explanation. The funny part was that they stopped bothering me for the money.

This, of course, was the period when I would stop strangers on the street or the bus and say, "My son died." I can't really explain why I did that. I certainly knew it was a crazy thing to do. I think that it was partly just a way to convince myself that it was true. Secretly I also loved the way it would totally horrify and deflate all those I stopped. I took a weird pleasure in ruining some poor slob's day—after all, my whole life had been ruined. Why not spread the pain around a little?

I also did something else, something typical for the time—I joined a self-help group. Compassionate Friends was meant for people who had lost a child. I know people who say this group saved them from going off the deep end. But while it works wonders for some, it didn't do it for me. I felt weird there—before the meeting, everyone would behave naturally, standing around in small groups, chatting about the weather and work and shopping and so on. Then the session would be called to order and one by one everybody took turns weeping and sharing their tales of woe. It was as if somebody had turned on the sprinkler system—the room was soaked in tears. It felt like you were expected to cry on command, which of course just made me determined to stay dry-eyed. When my turn to speak came, I said, "My name is Linda. My twenty-nine-year-old son was just killed in a car wreck. I don't like belonging to this club."

Things didn't improve much from there. During the meetings, as the other members spoke, all I could think was: *Why do I have to listen to you talk about how your child died? My child died!*

In other words, your problems are tedious, mine are compelling. Which is normal and natural and how it should be, let's be honest here. I didn't want to know about other people's dead kids—I still hadn't come to grips with my own dead kid.

I never went back. Before long I gave up the shrink too. I realized that just because we had suffered the same horrible loss didn't mean that she could help me get over it. I was a mother whose child had just died, but I was also a lot more than that. If the only qualification for helping me was the loss of a child, I would have had no shortage of help, believe me.

Finally, I attended something that would set me off on a voyage that's still going on. It was a lecture by Elisabeth Kübler-Ross. She's famous for death, of course—the author of *Death and Dying*, and the one who described to us exactly how and why we feel when we know we are about to die. Because of this lecture, my entire idea about death began to change.

Now, you should understand that before this I had no real ideas about death. To me, dead was dead. Certainly I had had enough people close to me die to know it was final, and it left you worse off than you had been before.

Suddenly, here's this woman, this expert, saying that you can't kill the human spirit. That the human spirit is energy, and it goes on existing after the body, the flesh, has died. I was filled with such hope, with the thought that maybe Jordan was still somewhere within reach. And this wasn't some airhead in a caftan with stars in her hair. This was a woman of science, a no-nonsense doctor in a drab polyester pants suit. If she had reason to believe that the energy of my son lived on, was still present in the world, who was I to doubt her? And let's be real, would any message have been more welcomed by me at that moment?

So—now I was looking at the strong (so it seemed) possibility that my son, or at least a very important part of him, was still at large in the world, unchanged by his passing. When I was agoraphobic, I devoured a book a day. It turned me into the kind of person who learns by reading as much as by seeing or hearing or experiencing. Now I was off and running, finding every book out there on the possibilities of life after death. I read religion. I read spirituality. I read the ancient wisdoms. I read the newest ones too. I read up on every *ism* I found. I even went back to my tattered Dr. Spock to see if there was something I had done wrong as a mother that led Jordan to die the way he did.

"Maybe if I hadn't yelled at him so much," I said to Robin. "Maybe I took away his pacifier too soon."

"What are you talking about?" she replied. "He didn't kill himself. He died in a car accident."

I actually had to be reminded of that. It was also at this time when, fearing for my sanity, I said to Robin, "I'm just afraid I'm going to go crazy and end up as one of those insane ladies who lives with forty-two cats and never opens a window." Robin looked at me with a level gaze and said patiently, "Mom, you hate cats."

At one point I was so desperate for sense that I consulted a rabbi.

"This is a terrible tragedy," he told me.

"Yes, Rabbi," I said.

"To lose a child is the worst loss."

"Yes, Rabbi."

"No one can say more than this."

And I sat there and thought: *For this I shlepped to New York from Queens on three buses?*

It's funny, not long before Jordan died I bought a book that was a best-seller at the time, *When Bad Things Happen to Good People*, by Rabbi Harold Kushner. I browsed a few pages, put it on a shelf, and forgot about it.

Then, after Jordan died and I began to devour any book I could find on spirituality and self-help, I stumbled over this one again in my bookcase. Naturally I took it down and began to read.

And once I read it I began to hate it. What the hell was this guy about? God made bad things happen to good people to teach them a lesson? I thought it was the most awful, hateful thing I had ever read. I was reading it on a bus, and was planning to toss it in the garbage at the first opportunity, when a woman sitting next to me says, "Oh, what's that you're reading?"

I spared her my feelings and just read the description off the book jacket.

"Gee, I could really use a book like that," she said.

"Here!" I exclaimed. "Take it, please!"

"Oh, no, I couldn't take your book while you're reading it," she said.

"Sure you could!" I replied. "Take it now!"

"Oh, but that wouldn't be right," she said.

"Yes it would," I said. "God put us here together for a reason. He wants you to have this book right now. He wants me to give it to you."

As you can tell, none of the old religions were of much use to me during this time of my life. So I ended up inventing a new one, called Lindaism. In Lindaism, I reached around me and grabbed anything that looked the least bit helpful. I was a drowning woman, grasping at straws, reeds, ropes, and anything else within my reach. And because all this took place when it did—in the early '90s—my new faith borrowed quite a bit from another nontraditional form of spirituality that was in the air.

I went slightly New Age.

Now, I imagine that most people get into this a little at a time. You're curious, you read up on it, you think it over, you talk to somebody, you watch *Oprah*, one thing leads to another, and you absorb it into your life at a deliberate pace. You don't get too far ahead of yourself.

Of course, that wasn't going to be my way. Because I was in such dire need that I needed a lot of help in a hurry. I didn't have time to think long and hard.

So the first thing I did was start going to lectures and workshops and seminars and anything else like that. In the first year after Jordan died, I went to 103 lectures. That's better than two a week. That's Saturday, Sunday, and maybe a Wednesday night. You name it, I went. I had no idea which one was going to help, which one would provide me with a little respite from the pain, so I had to go to them all. I was indiscriminate. Deepak? I was there. Shakti Gawain? Right up front. I can't even remember most of them, which is a blessing in itself, believe me. If it was spirituality, if it was self-help, if it promised the secret to a life of peace and tranquillity, I was in the room.

It may sound as though I was flying without a flight plan, but even then some force was directing me where I needed to go.

Just after Jordan died a friend gave me a book titled *You'll See It When You Believe It*, by Dr. Wayne W. Dyer, who was best known for having written *Your Erroneous Zones*, a book that has sold millions of copies. All I knew about the book was that it was termed "pop psychology." And the last thing I needed, I told my friend, was a pop psychologist. I had just lost a son! I needed something a little more substantial, I said.

And then, one night maybe a week later, I couldn't sleep. Coincidentally, *You'll See It When You Believe It* was lying on my nightstand. So I turned on the light, grabbed it, and started to read, praying that it would bore me to sleep. Instead I discovered the first thing to give me hope in that bleak time of my life. This book just had the most profound effect imaginable on me. It said things simply and powerfully, and the fact that the author didn't try to seem deep or philosophical made him all the more convincing. His words of hope and help just stuck in my soul.

A short while later my friend said that Dr. Dyer was going to be lecturing in New York, and did I want to go? Of course I went, not as a fan but as someone who needed— needed—to hear an intelligent, sane, believable message. I didn't need anything too woo-woo. I didn't need anybody making promises and claims so spectacular that my skepticism would be aroused. I just needed to hear something straight and true that might help me through a devastating crisis.

The lecture was everything I'd hoped it would be. When it was over my friend asked if I wanted to see if we could meet Dr. Dyer. Sure, I said, let's try. At the stage exit of the Paramount Theater, where the lecture was held, there was already a small mob of people waiting. Dr. Dyer emerged and began signing autographs. He was encircled by admirers, and I was maybe eight or nine people away from him—a good distance, considering the crush.

But then he suddenly looked up into the crowd, straight into my eyes. A moment later he motioned with his hand for me to step to one side. Then the crowd parted and he walked over to speak to me.

"What's wrong?" he asked, just like that. I mean, I wasn't weeping or anything. He just looked and knew the depth of my pain.

"My son just died," I said.

"Let's talk," he said. We talked for a few minutes, and in that time my belief in the power of his message was confirmed.

I still have the same copy of his book, ten years later. I've read it more times than I can count—I'm always picking it up and reading it, a few chapters at a time. I read this book the way some people read the Bible—as a constant and ongoing project, always finding something new with each passage. Without exaggeration I've given away scores of copies, but my old dog-eared book will always be with me. This book has told me so many things, more than I can even summarize here. When we spoke that night and I said my son had died, he replied that he didn't know how he would handle such a tragedy, and that he knew it must be hard, but that someday I would know the reason it happened. And he was right.

I also discovered a little New Age bookstore in Forest Hills, Queens. I began buying and reading books by the armload. I read voraciously, but only books by gurus, therapists, channelers, psychics, spirit guides, and anyone else who claimed to be able to help me. To this day I have never met anyone who has consumed as much of the self-help section of the bookstore as I have. I continue reading that and nothing else.

At that little shop I also began my collection of crystals and rocks and stones and relics. And candles and incense. And little plaster angels. Everything in the store supposedly had meaning and power, and if there was anything I desperately needed at the time, it was meaning and power. So I bought it all and believed completely in whatever claims the various trinkets and talismans made.

A purple stone is for healing? It went right into my pocket, and it stayed there. Did I have any objective reason for believing that a purple stone held any power whatsoever? No. But—did I have any proof that it *wouldn't* help? Aha! So I carried it, because what if?

Prosperity incense? If it really had the power to bring prosperity to all those who burn it, wouldn't I have heard something about it by now? Wouldn't I know at least one or two incense-burning billionaires? That's not how I thought about it. I figured, look, it's called prosperity incense, and there must be a reason! Somebody must know more than me about it, because I know absolutely nothing!

Maybe once upon a time I would have had my bull detector on, and I would have laughed at the very thought of this stuff. Now though, I had been unhinged by grief. You can become so desperate for something to believe in that you'll believe in anything. You don't spend too much time analyzing—you just grab hard and hang on! In that state of mind you don't have the luxury of taking your time or thinking things through or being careful not to make a fool of yourself. Looking back I can laugh. At the time, there was nothing funny. But neither was there anything wrong with my search for meaning. The fact is that if you are honestly looking for the path to sanity and happiness, you'll find it. I had to do all the kooky things I did to get to where I am today. For that reason alone, they weren't so kooky. I advise people I know to go after wisdom the same way—with an open heart and not too much worry about looking foolish. It's only foolish not to try.

For instance, I'd come home from the lectures I attended on fire with the wisdom I learned. I'd be bursting with spiritual insights. Lots of times I'd try and get my sister Judy and her husband Sid in on my latest thing. I remember dragging them along to hear some healer who specialized in treating people with AIDS. They were absolutely appalled by what they saw—from their perspective I had dragged them to witness a charlatan taking advantage of some very sick people. I was sure that they just didn't get it—their eyes weren't open enough to truly take in what was there before them.

And the tapes! Lots of soft, monotone voices, repeating the same affirmations over and over, while wind chimes tinkled in the background. I love myself, the universe loves me, I love the universe . . . if you ever watched Al Franken do Stuart Smalley on *Saturday Night Live*, you laughed at what you thought was a parody, but take it from me—it wasn't far from the truth. The thing with the tapes wasn't so much that they gave you new wisdom or information— just playing the damn things over and over again was supposed to be how they worked their magic. So those tapes were the soundtrack of my life. They were on not just during my waking hours but when I slept too.

(I truly believe, even now, that those tapes could permeate my soul while I slept. Because as a kid, after my father died, I couldn't sleep. I developed childhood insomnia. So my mother figured that maybe if she left the radio on in my room it would help me to sleep. Back then Barry Gray was *the* nighttime radio god in New York. So that's who I tuned in. As a result, I became a talk radio junkie, an addiction I maintain to this day. And I know you can absorb radio even while you sleep because my brain is filled with facts that I picked up in the middle of the night thanks to Barry Gray. I absorbed the craziest collection of trivia thanks to that man, and I manage to impress friends and acquaintances all the time because of him. When he died a few years ago, it was like I lost a relative. I cried like a baby, because I had spent forty years listening to him.)

I was a receiver of wisdoms then, no matter where they

came from. I was reeling from my son's death, an open wound. The people who come to my lectures and workshops today are a lot like I was back when I went to a different lecture or seminar every week. I was a wounded bird, a cripple, and all I wanted was for somebody to tell me how to get better. I wanted somebody to say, "Linda, honey, click your heels, repeat the words 'There's no place like home' three times, and everything will be all right." Except there ain't no such shoes. There's no magic. If there was, everybody would know about it and there'd be no need for lectures or therapists or spirituality workshops or self-help books. The fact that so many people claim to have the universal answer just means that nobody has it. There is no answer. There are no ruby slippers. There are no magic words.

I actually have a weird thing where magic is concerned. I hate magicians and magic acts. To me, the true meaning of the phrase "Now you see it, now you don't" is this: "I know what just happened and you haven't got a clue, you idiot." I feel insulted by magic acts. For some strange reason, it hits a nerve. It makes me mad. Part of that is the trickery of sleight of hand, the secrecy, but the rest is just my overall suspicion of magic words and quick and easy solutions.

I spent a lot of time and money and effort tracking down the magic words, as spoken by the all-wise guru. If they were out there, I would have stumbled over them. Remember, this is somebody who attended two or three lectures and seminars *a week* for over a year. I still have yet to find anybody who's read as many self-help and spirituality books as me. I've learned something from nearly every one, but in none of them did I learn everything. So I'm not coming to you as a spirituality expert—I'm a seeker too, just like you. I read all the books and listened to the tapes and clutched the crystals in my sweaty little palms. Take it from me: There's no quick fix.

And to be honest, that suits me fine. As bad off as I was, as confused and crazed by grief and loss, I never felt completely comfortable with the notion that there was a miracle solution somewhere out there. I've always been a very practical, down-to-earth person. I credit a lot of that to growing up in Queens. Queens is not the mystical center of the planet. Queens is not Sedona, Arizona. Nobody traipses down Queens Boulevard in a flowing silk caftan. The only chanting in Queens is done at Shea Stadium when the Mets are home.

When anybody experiences a devastating loss, they want to find the sense in it. We all go around thinking life should make sense. There's supposed to be a reason for everything, especially something like that. It's too terrifying to think such a thing could happen for no reason at all.

Was there a reason my son died? The more I thought about that question, the less I even understood what it meant. *A reason?* I wanted to find something that would fit the definition of that word, as in: There's a reason I ate lunch—I was hungry. There's a reason the vase broke—it fell off the table. Something concrete like that.

But what possible reason could there be for my son to die? Did the universe, in all its power and glory, actually require the presence of Jordan's energy field elsewhere? Maybe something broke somewhere in the fourth dimension and my son was the only soul in all of existence who knew how to fix it? Maybe the universe was a little too crowded with earthly beings at that moment, and so my son (along with whoever else died that day) had to clear out? That makes sense, doesn't it? That's a reason.

Okay, let's cut the nonsense.

You want a reason my son died? Try this: He was being stupid that day and didn't wear his seat belt! How's that for a reason? Is that otherworldly enough for you? Does it ring all your spiritual chimes? If the universe really had a reason for my son dying when and how he did, it would be a universe too stupid and senseless to exist for a week. A universe that ridiculous couldn't manage to keep the sun up in the sky two days in a row.

So please don't think there was a reason he died other than the reason everybody dies, which is that he stopped living. One second he was alive and the next second something came along and changed that. Happens to the nicest people. If it hasn't happened to you yet, don't worry, it will. When Jordan came into existence I didn't go around asking gurus, "Why was he born? What's the reason? There *must* be a reason!" I knew the reason babies are born, and so do you. Nothing could be more basic than the start of life. And there's nothing more basic than the end of it. When you consider all the hazards that we face every single day, it's practically a miracle that anybody lives to be two.

Now then, if you want to talk about the reasons I can *invent* to bring meaning to my son's death, then pull up a chair. We've got a good long discussion ahead of us.

Here's one thing I learned about life from my son's death: Life has what meaning we give it. No more. No less. You are the only one who can give your life meaning, so if you're looking for it, start looking there—at yourself. Everything that happens to you will mean what you make it mean. It's up to you. I could have simply remained in misery after my son died, suffering and grieving and searching in vain for answers where none exist. I could have moped through every day until my own death came, at which point it would feel like a blessing.

Or I could have chosen an alternative.

Meaning what? Meaning that I could decide what meaning my son's death would have. I could *give* it a meaning. Because if I didn't give it one, it would never have one.

And it was at about this point in the journey when I gave up on gurus. I gave up on finding a road map in somebody else's book. If there was a God, he or she or it was already in me. If there was a path, I already knew it.

12 "Coffee Talk" or Me?

Mom," my daughter said on the phone, "I met your son-in-law last night."

This was maybe thirteen years ago.

"How great!" I said. "Where?"

"In a bar."

Could be worse, I thought.

"Tell me more."

"He's a foreigner," she said.

Ooh, now this might be tricky. My immediate thought? Exchange student from the Middle East. Meet my son-in-law the Arab terrorist.

"And he's in show business."

An Arab terrorist who will never make a decent living. This was the man my only daughter wanted to marry.

"And *where* did you say he's from?" I said, closing my eyes, clenching my jaws, and holding my breath.

"Canada," she said.

Whew! Is Canada a foreign country?

"What kind of show business?"

"He's a comic," she said.

So he'll never earn a decent living, I was right on that count. And in fact, at the time he was this little WASPy shlepper from Toronto working with the Second City comedy troupe in Chicago, making maybe a hundred bucks a week.

But he was without a doubt the most lovable and adorable little WASPy shlepper from Canada I had ever met. So of course once I got to know Mike I saw what Robin saw and thanked my lucky stars.

One day I went to their apartment. He answered the door.

"So, where's my daughter?" I asked.

"Where's your dawtuh?" he said.

"Yes, where's my daughter?"

"She's in the kitchen having cawfey," he replied.

"Having cawfey?"

"Yes, your dawtuh's in the kitchen having cawfey with the dawg."

He went on that way. And not just for that moment—he began to impersonate me whenever I was around. For all I know he impersonated me even when I wasn't around. Before long he did me better than I did. That's what happens when there's a comedian in the family.

So comes a time he gets his first big break, ta-dah, and now he's a regular cast member of *Saturday Night Live.* The big time.

One day he comes to me and says, "Linda, I want to do you on the show."

"Are you crazy?" I said. "You can't do me on network TV. Nobody in Kansas is going to get me. Nobody in Iowa is going to get me. You're going to do me and it's going to be a huge bust and they're going to fire you."

I'm looking out for my daughter, not to mention my future unborn grandchildren.

It would be very funny, he said. Everybody would love it. So I gave him my blessing—oh, maybe I was just the tiniest bit flattered—and prepared for the worst.

Because I am such a proud mother-in-law, I went to every show back then. One night I'm mingling backstage beforehand and I notice that Mike's friends are behaving strangely toward me. Like there's something they're hiding.

And then I see me. I mean him. Big black bouffant hairdo. Beaded sweater. Huge eyeglasses. Leather pants. Nails out to here.

I have to admit, it was pretty close. The wardrobe looked like he had been through my closet.

"Linda!" he yelled when he saw me. "You are stunning! You are a stunnah!"

"No, you are a stunnah!" I yelled back.

And the show went on, and my astuteness when it comes to comedy proved itself once again. He was a huge hit, and people from coast to coast loved the bit. Before long the word "shpilkas" was being uttered in places where it had never been uttered before, as was the word "buttah." And did somebody say "fahrklempt"?

Once, not long after, in Wisconsin, I met this real uptight church lady type. Tight gray curls, the whole prissy Midwest Presbyterian thing. We start talking and I tell her Mike's my son-in-law and I'm the real Linda Richman.

"Oh my God," she said, smiling. "I am so fahrklempt to meet you! My entire church group watches you every time without fail!"

This is nuts, I thought. This makes no sense. Jews loved the character, but that I could understand. Every Jew in New York came up to me and said, "You're exactly like my Aunt Yetta!" So if you love Aunt Yetta, you love Linda Richman. But there are no Aunt Yettas in Wisconsin. And they got it too.

When Mike created the character, he asked if he could give her my actual name. Sure, I said, with pleasure, thinking, oh, isn't this amusing? and having no idea how it would catch on. Soon I'd be going about my life as normal, only now every time I said my name, practically, I'd get this:

"No . . . wait . . . are you . . . ?"

Yes, I'd have to admit. I am the real . . .

You can imagine. Once in a while would have been nice. But this was constant. Before long I hated to buy anything, because once I handed over my credit card, they'd read the name and say:

"No . . . wait . . . are you . . . ?"

I began lying. Even worse, I changed my last name, just to avoid being stopped two or three or twelve times a day.

Of course, it was a kick, all in all. After the character had really caught on, Mike got a call one day from Barbra Streisand. She was about to go on an eight-city tour, and she wanted to know would he do a guest appearance at the concerts in Linda Richman drag?

Sure, he said, with one condition. My mother-in-law has to get tickets to every concert.

Heaven! I became the oldest groupie in America. Not only did I get to hear her sing for eight unforgettable shows, I even got to meet her!

Beyond that brush with fame, I had calls to appear on TV shows and in magazine and newspaper articles, but I turned them down. I had one big fear in my head: Jackie Stallone. The last thing I wanted was to be a famous mother-in-law.

And this kept me cautious about my new, weird brand

of fame. I was the most famous unknown person in America, I used to think.

I was perfectly content that way too.

But there's more. (There's always more.) The custom back then was that after *Saturday Night Live*, the cast and their friends (and relatives, sometimes) would gather in Lorne Michaels's office. There, one night, I met a young guy named Michael. And we're talking and shmoozing, the same as everybody else around us, and I take a backseat to no one in the talking and shmoozing department. I don't care how famous or accomplished they may be.

So we're laughing, and may I say that Michael is a gay man, which is an added incentive to the conversation because gay men love me, and I love them. I am the fag hag of all time, pardon the expression.

Suddenly Michael says that he produces TV shows and he wants to put together a talk show with me as the host.

Now, you know and I know that a big part of his reasoning must have been that here I was, already famous and loved by millions, at least in proxy form. Thanks to Mike, I was already the star of a talk show—"Coffee Talk." So how much of a leap was it to say, Hey, let's take that bit from *Saturday Night Live* and run with it?

And it's not like he was taking a tree stump and turning it into a talk show host.

A talk show? Oh, of course, what a fabulous idea, I said. All the while thinking: Typical Hollywood bull. Everybody is a star, baby. I love it, I tell him, let's do it right away. And then I completely forget about it. Out of my mind.

A few weeks go by and the phone rings and it's Michael and dimly I remember meeting him.

"William Morris wants to represent you," he says.

"Excuse me?" I say.

"For the show," he says. "They want to fly you out here."

"Sure," I say, "tell William to call me!"

Next day, William calls. In the course of a single phone call they offer to represent me, explain the terms of our contract, and let me know when my flight leaves and which fancy hotel will be graced with my presence.

Did I go? Are you kidding?

Short story—I get there, and boom, we're making the pilot for *The Linda Richman Show*. We have offices. We have an executive producer, a line producer, an associate producer, producers everywhere you turn. In the lobby of the building, on the directory, there it is: *The Linda Richman Show*.

It's real, isn't it?

Not only that, but they're paying me $25,000 for three months' work, if you can call it that. Even better, if the show actually ever gets on the air I'll make $3 million the first year and $5 million the second year, and escalating this and sliding that and all I can think is: I'll never be homeless again.

Forget for the moment that I never was homeless before. In my head I was always one false step away from sleeping inside an old refrigerator box.

So I've gone Hollywood! But me in Hollywood is still the same me as me in Queens. Meaning that even at the center of this hive of fabulousness, all I can think is: This is just absurd. None of this is based on anyone's long familiarity with my abilities as an entertainer, which happen to be nonexistent. It's all about the me as created by Mike. So my son-in-law impersonates me doing a TV talk show. Next thing you know, I'm impersonating him impersonating me doing a TV talk show.

So I don't believe any of it. But at the same time I'm gung ho full speed ahead.

And we're building up to the big day—the taping of

the pilot. If the audience likes me, if the suits like me, if the advertisers like me, if the station owners like me, then we have a show.

Normally a talk show pilot is a fairly low-key thing. They're auditioning the host, not the guests. So you'll get Joe Shmo as your big name. But for me, of course, the obvious choice is—get Mike Myers! Could he say no? No! They knew that Rosie O'Donnell was one of my dear friends. Could she say no? No! Then they called in Maria Shriver and a few others, and before you know it we've got one hell of a pilot we're putting on.

And then two things happen. One is that my mother dies. For better or worse, the figure who looms largest in my life, and especially my nightmares, is no longer among the living. But the show must go on! I can't even sit shiva properly because the show must go on. So I skip the ritual of mourning, which makes the actual mourning that much worse. Inside, I'm a basket case.

The other thing is that it finally begins to dawn on the big shots just what they have on their hands. They wanted the real Linda Richman, they wanted the actual human being who inspired the Mike Myers character, but once they had me, they realized something—I was the real Linda Richman. With the emphasis on real. I was not a showbiz confection. I didn't put on Linda Richman every morning like makeup or a costume. I was really me all the time.

Which maybe, it suddenly hit them, wasn't exactly the stuff of the TV talk shows they were used to producing. They wanted haimish, which means, for you goyim out there, down-to-earth, unpretentious, homemade. They wanted that until they got it.

I was getting little hints that that was the case. I was getting the vague sense that maybe I was a little too much me.

By the day of the taping, I was in a stone cold panic, wondering what in the hell ever gave me the idea that I could be a TV talk show host. The studio is freezing. I'm sweating and shvitzing under the lights and in my own wild-eyed fear. The audience is in the chairs. The cameras are on. The band is playing. The countdown has begun.

Five . . . four . . . three . . .

And at that moment, the biggest bigwig leans over and whispers in my ear. Here's what he says:

"Don't be too Jewish."

I'm dead! I'm buried! What should I be? If I ain't Jewish, I ain't breathing. Who did this schmuck think he hired—Lynn Redgrave? Let's put aside for the moment the fact that the executive who whispered this in my ear is as Jewish as I am. I mean, this is maybe the nastiest thing that I have ever heard by somebody who wasn't intending to insult me. Let's focus instead on the fact that the rest of the countdown has been counted down, the announcer has just screamed my name, and we're live on tape!

Only where's the camera? And where's the cue card girl? I knew those damn cards were going to give me trouble, but the execs said you can't do a show without them. During the rehearsal the cue card girl was right where I could find her, to my immediate left. Or was it my immediate right? I can't see her anywhere, and even if I could there's no guarantee I would be able to say the right words, because while I'm frantically scanning the set, there's a voice yelling in my ear. It's yelling things like, "Camera right! Camera right!" And I'm swiveling my head like a maniac, all the while with a grin of sheer terror frozen on my face.

Can you tell I was uncomfortable?

I'm not even going to tell you what the rest of the show was like. In truth, it got better. I asked my questions, not the ones on the cue cards, and thank God I had true pros like Mike and Rosie and Maria to carry me that day. I make it through the taping, return to the dressing room, and begin to cry my eyes out. Even the industrial-strength mascara they had on me was no match for the torrent of tears that ensued. You know, I went along with this TV scheme because it was fun and even a little flattering. But at no time did I believe that I had somehow been reborn as a genuine TV personality. Neither was I interested in changing anything about myself to fit the notions of these Hollywood guys. Sitting in that host's chair, I realized fulfilling other people's expectations—no matter how flattering they are—paves the road to disappointment.

Which turns out to have been a good thing. A minute after the taping ends, Michael, who had gotten my whole TV career going, enters my dressing room.

"Listen to me," I sob. "I don't care what anybody says, I'm not doing this."

"Don't worry," he consoles me. "They *hated* you!"

13 More Travels in the Spirit World

Let me tell you about two further jaunts into the realm of the Great Whatever, each of which started with my old pal Richard suggesting a simple little vacation. Just to show that when you're meant to spend time in a weird place, nothing is going to stop you.

The first one I can't even call a vacation. It was a quick, harmless jaunt. How did we choose Sedona, Arizona? Neither Richard nor I had ever even heard of the place, let alone its reputation. It was part of an extremely cheap package trip that would give him some good golfing in the hot, dry Southwest, and me a little shopping and sunbathing. We knew from Phoenix. We knew from Tucson. Sedona? Part of the package.

So we get there. I had just left my husband. Richard had been divorced for some time. I am in my forties. He's in his sixties. I'm just beginning my search for spiritual meaning in life, but barely. My son's still alive and well at this point, so I'm in no burning need for comfort in a cold, uncaring universe. Richard is a retired salesman, meaning he believes in nothing he can't see, taste, smell, or touch. When it comes to religion or spirituality, to Richard it's all bull. That's what he believes.

So even when we arrive in Sedona neither one of us has the slightest idea that it is supposed to be this great place of healing and spirituality. We have no idea that pilgrims from all over the world flock to this sacred spot in the desert. We're here for the golfing and the shopping and that's it.

Why did I wonder about psychics once we got to town? To this day I can't say for sure. All I know is that we settled in and first thing I asked the clerk at the hotel was whether there were any psychics in Sedona.

"Everybody is a psychic in Sedona," he said.

"Are they listed in the Yellow Pages?" I asked. And sure enough they were.

What did I hope to get out of it? Not much. Back then I had a parlor game of clipping the horoscope page from the newspaper, whiting out the zodiac signs, and seeing if any of my friends could pick theirs. Nobody could, to my delight.

Anyway, I look at the listings and there I see one named Marcy Abraham. I chose her solely because her name sounded Jewish. I was going to visit the only Jewish psychic in Sedona, Arizona.

Well, of course, she wasn't Jewish at all—she was this skinny little redheaded Southern Baptist.

"Richard, do you want to come in with me?" I asked him.

"Sure, why not," he said. Couldn't care one way or the other.

We go in and sit.

"Just tell me your birth date," she says.

I tell her.

"I have to say," she starts, "that I love your wedding ring."

"Thanks," I say.

"But you're not married to him." She gives Richard the eye.

"How do you know?" I say. We never said a thing.

"How do I know?" she says. "I know everything. I know you left your husband not long ago, and that this man has been in your life for a very long time, since you were a little girl."

Okay, now I'm hooked. No way she could know that Richard was an old family friend. I made a tape of our session and I only wish I could find it today. Part of me believes now that what she said about me could also be said of most women. But part of me still wonders.

By the end of the session she had blown my mind. Even Richard didn't know what to think.

"I'm coming to New York," Marcy says to me. "If you get me three clients up there, I'll give you a free reading when I'm in town."

"Three?" I say. "I can do a whole lot better than that."

I went home and called everybody I knew. By the time she hit town, I had lined up forty readings for her. Before long she was coming to New York once a month—the forty people I had lined up led to lots more clients, and she ended up pretty well-known among New York ladies who believe in psychics. I'd even send out letters announcing her visits, and she had quite a practice in a hurry.

She never charged me a nickel after that, and it was a good thing, because I had become hooked on Marcy. But she never took advantage, and she became my good friend in addition to being my spiritual adviser. I got to where I wouldn't make a move without consulting with her.

I'd call her up with some dilemma, some big choice I was facing.

"Marcy, what should I do?" I'd ask.

"What does your heart tell you to do?" she'd reply.

"Well, my heart tells me yes," I'd say.

"That's the answer I have for you too," she'd respond after a meaningful pause.

And guess what? Her advice was always right! Isn't it amazing how wise someone can sound when they tell you to do the very thing you really want to do? I'm being just the tiniest bit sarcastic here, but the truth is that she gave me tremendous confidence. I always chose right when I followed her "advice"—largely because she gave me the courage and the belief in myself to do what I set out to do. Without her psychic guidance, I might have done the same things, only without the full belief in my ability to pull it off. And maybe then I would have flopped. So is that psychic power or is it not?

For instance, she helped a great deal as I established my own business. I was just starting then, and was barely getting enough jobs to keep me busy. When I did get a job, I charged so little that there was no profit even after a lot of hard work.

"If people think you work cheap," she told me, "they'll never want you."

"What do you mean?" I asked.

"If you're cheap you can't be good. Overcharge them and they'll be beating down your door."

I was afraid that following her advice would put me out of business altogether. Back then the going rate for the big outfits in my field was around $3,000 a day. I was asking $500, I explained, figuring that I'd win clients on price if nothing else.

"Charge $3,500 a day," Marcy told me.

"You're crazy," I said. "I can't get that."

"Do it," she advised me, with all the authority of the stars and the planets and the celestial forces on her side.

So I did it, and she was right! Who knew the heavens were so smart about the casting business?

She was right about everything else she told me too. It was Marcy who started me in my reading on spirituality, sending books (without charge) that filled me in on exactly why the universe was suddenly working for me instead of against. Not woo-woo books either—well, maybe a few of those—but mostly books of genuine value to me then. Books I still read to this day. When Marcy came into my life things just began getting better. Is it any wonder I connected the two?

Then my world fell to pieces when my son died. But Marcy too had lost a child—a daughter who had died thirteen years earlier. When Jordan was killed I called Marcy and she came running up to New York to be with me. Once again, I found proof of how the universe was providing for my well-being. Marcy's presence in my life at that moment was a blessing.

In fact, she actually helped conduct the service at Jordan's funeral. The rabbi was thrilled, as you can imagine—he had to share the podium with this skinny lady in a white coat with stars in her hair. But there's no way I would have gotten through it without her.

She remained a major part of my life for the next couple years too. I called her all the time, and our conversations gave me strength. I have to laugh at it now, because she was right out of the trailer park, and I was hanging on every word like she was the Dalai Lama. And can you blame me? It worked! She was my first tour guide to the spirit world. And while it seems funny today, I never would have gotten there without her.

After a while she decided that she wanted to start conducting workshops in New York, so I helped establish that for her—I got dozens of women to pay $100 or so each for a day under Marcy's spell. She taught us relaxation, guided imagery, meditation—tools I use to this day to help keep me on an even keel. She also performed some past life regressions, which was totally insane, let's be real here. But when you're ready to go insane, that was a pretty good way to go. Who were you? Oh, I was a flapper! I was Queen Victoria! Cleopatra! Why the hell not?

I'm no longer looking into the mists of history to figure out who I am or how I got here. It made sense for a while, but that while is past, thank God. Marcy's no longer in my life either. As someone wise once told me, a guru shouldn't be a guru for more than two weeks.

That entire chapter of my life is funny today, mainly because it was so extremely out there. But all of it, especially Marcy, was exactly what I needed for my first step on the spiritual highway, and I always say this: You take your wisdom where you find it.

For instance, one of the wisest things I ever heard was this: People need three things in life—someone to love, something to love, and something to look forward to.

Do you know where it comes from? That great sage and holy figure Kenny Rogers, the country singer. Do I wish I could say, I found those words in the *Tibetan Book of the Dead* or some other awe-inspiring place? I sure do. But it just happens that ol' Kenny was the one who said them. Between Marcy and Kenny, I've learned a lot and felt a lot better. Do you need more proof that God works in strange ways?

The second fateful vacation happened not long after my son died. Richard suggested this one too, and in the course of my search for spiritual meaning and inner peace it made perfect sense. So I went to Israel.

Now, me being a major-league yenta, Israel might not seem like such a weird choice for my travels. It's not beyond the realm of possibility that I might find some tranquillity there. A million pilgrims can't be completely wrong.

On the other hand, I am not the most observant Jew in the world. My mother grew up in a Catholic convent orphanage, remember, which didn't exactly turn her into a devout little mameleh. I was enrolled in Hebrew school, but instead of going I usually went to the five-and-dime with my friend Ellen. All those Jews with long beards scared me. Given the choice between the Holy Land and, say, Paris, I'd be on the Concorde faster than you can say Golda Meir.

In fact, the only reason I was going to Israel was that my old friend Richard had found a package deal for an irresistible price. It was almost cheaper to go to Israel than it was to stay home. So we went.

Of course, me being me, I knew that there had to be a bigger reason for this trip. There are no accidents in the universe, I figured, so I'd be on the lookout. Plus, everybody around me thought it was a great idea. I'd get off the plane, fall to my knees, and kiss the ground, they guaranteed.

And then we landed in Tel Aviv and I looked around and thought: Miami Beach. But without the Fountainbleu. I spent a few days there, got bored out of my skull, and felt no better about anything. So I moved on to Jerusalem.

No sooner am I there than I begin sightseeing, come to the top of a hill, and spot a sign that says: Jordan River. My son's name, of course, is Jordan. So I see it and suddenly I think, "What's the meaning of *this?*"

I had no idea that Jordan the country was Israel's next-door neighbor, so I'd be seeing signs with my son's name on them every time I turned around. It was Jordan River this way, and Jordan Mountains over there, and to the left to Jordan, over and over. Constant reminders of my son. I mean overload.

Just to catch my breath, I thought I would do what all Jews do when they come to Israel. They plant trees.

Why do Jews plant trees? Beats the hell out of me. Outside of Israel, has a Jew ever planted a tree? I don't believe so. You have to dig in the woods, and Jews don't dig in the woods. They don't go camping either. Jews don't fix cars. Jews don't go hunting. Jews don't stick up bank tellers or gas stations. They don't go to jail for murder. Once, I visited a friend of a friend at the federal prison in Danbury, Connecticut. He was there for income tax evasion. Jews *do* income tax evasion! This was an entire prison for income tax cheats—a jail for Jews!

Anyway. In Israel you go and there's a guy who sells you saplings, and lends you a hoe, and he takes you into the forest and shows you where to dig, and you dig a little and put the tree in there and wipe off your hands and you're a good Jew. But I asked him to just drive me into the forest and leave me there with a dozen saplings but no hoe. And I told him to leave me alone for an hour and then come back.

What was my plan? I had no idea. I only knew that I wanted to be alone, and that somehow I thought that if I used my hands instead of a hoe to dig the holes, I would be that much closer to whatever the hell I was trying to find.

So I began to dig. And pray. Keep in mind, I don't actually know any prayers. Instead, I begin speaking directly to my son. Tender things, like, "Jordan, what the hell was wrong with you? Why didn't you wear a seat belt, you goddamn idiot?!" And I'm digging and scratching at the earth, and I'm yelling and screaming, so that before long I'm crying too. Hysterically crying. There was nothing funny about this. It was one of the most painful moments of my life, in fact.

And then I saw in a flash how I would have looked to anyone passing by—there, alone in the middle of a forest, was a chunky middle-aged Jewish woman from Queens, surrounded by saplings, screaming and crying and cursing and destroying her manicure. Does life get any more absurd than that? If you had come upon me, would you have done anything but laugh your head off?

That's exactly what I started to do. By then I had cried myself out, so laughter was all I had left. It was at this moment that my sapling salesman chose to return for me. He rushed to my side once he heard me, because he was convinced that I was weeping so hard I would hurt myself.

It was cathartic, as you might imagine. I felt quite a bit lighter when I left that forest. But this was not the end of my grand religious experiences in the Holy Land. No, I had yet to take the final plunge.

A day or so later, I'm riding in a taxi by the Jordan River when I see a sign announcing the schedule of baptisms. But of course! My little tree-hugging episode wasn't why the spirit world had drawn me to Israel. I was meant to reunite with my son by immersing myself in the Jordan! Forget about whether I'm about to commit an act so sacrilegious that I'll be condemned to the fiery pit of hell for two or three eternities.

So I stop the taxi and approach the chief guy. I don't know whether I'm supposed to call him Father or Reverend or what. I know I can't fall back on "Hey, Rabbi."

"Your Honor?" I said.

"Yes?" he replied.

"I have a question."

"Yes?"

"I am Jewish top to bottom, inside and out, but I want to be baptized in the Jordan River."

"Thirty-five shekels," he replied.

Okay! This I understand.

And that's how I was baptized, may all the world's Jews, living and dead, forgive me. There I stood among hundreds of gentiles with their crucifixes and rosary beads and me in my designer cruisewear. I got in line, paid my money, and was dunked right alongside all my new Christian brothers and sisters.

I raced back to the hotel to tell my daughter the good news. Because of the time difference, we communicated daily through faxes rather than phone calls. So I sat down and wrote what had happened that day, and that I even had a new Christian name, and that henceforth she should call me Muffy. Look, if I was going to go gentile, I was going to go all the way.

14 You Talkin' to Me?

On the one hand, I want to be a realistic person.

On the other, there's such a thing as too realistic.

I especially don't want to be too realistic on the negative side of things. I can invent plenty of negative thoughts on my own. I don't need reality adding any to the party.

For instance, my thing used to be that I'd call myself stupid. If I dropped a glass, I'd say, "Oh, how stupid!" Or if I said something wrong, I'd berate myself later: "How could you be so stupid?"

It wasn't that I liked being called stupid. In fact, I hated it. In fact, it was (and still is) the one insult I hate above all others.

This is a result of my mother having called me stupid when I was a child. Now, I was not a stupid child, and my mother was not a stupid woman, therefore she knew I was actually a pretty smart kid. That I never heard from her. Stupid, I heard. If I dropped something. If my child's logic led me to a wrong conclusion.

Even back then I became angry when she'd call me that.

As an adult that didn't change, except it was me I was getting angry at. I go into a rage today if someone even implies that I'm stupid.

Still, I'd miss an exit on the highway:

"Stupid!"

Or I'd get on the wrong bus:

"Stupid!"

I'd end up feeling stupid and angry simultaneously, which did wonders for my disposition.

Once I started reading spiritual books, that began to change. In practically every self-help book you can find, you'll read the same thing: Be nice to yourself. Don't undermine yourself. Don't fill your head with negativity.

Okay, it's not the most original insight you'll ever hear, but it makes sense, right? There are probably already enough people who think you are stupid.

So I changed my ways.

I missed an exit?

"Oh, will you look at that? Well—no harm done!"

I dropped a glass?

"Uh-oh, better get the mop!"

I still did all the missing and dropping I ever did. But I stopped judging myself harshly for it. People miss exits! Glasses drop! Does it have to mean I'm stupid? Why, of course not!

This realization came during a period when I was experiencing moments of tremendous, knee-knocking insight the way some people experience gas—another outbreak every twenty minutes or so. This was, as I fondly remember it, my woo-woo stage. Imagine someone who is spiritual to the extreme. Now keep going. That was me.

Before long, I refused to call *anybody* stupid, no matter what they said or did. If filling my brain with negative thoughts about myself was no good, how could negative thoughts about other people be much better?

I became a saint. St. Linda of Forest Hills.

If I was walking down the street and somebody spit on me, I'd say, "Bless you!" Where before, if somebody spit on me, I'd spit back. Everything was lovely, and everybody was a child of God, and la la la la la. I was Mother Teresa, in love with the universe and everything in it. Oh, I was glorious. Everybody I met was the most treasured and blessed and celestial person in the world. Every minute I spent with someone was the most fulfilling, exalted, life-affirming moment of my existence. I was nuts, in other words. I was so good I was insane. Not one little negative thought was going to sneak into my brain.

During this period, perhaps not coincidentally, I found myself the target of one of the craziest human beings I've ever known in my life. I can't print every detail here because she'd recognize herself and I don't want to give her an excuse to contact me ever again. Back then, she believed, quite incorrectly, that I had wronged her. And so she sued me. Not once. Not twice. She'd sue me maybe every month or so. It got to where I knew the process servers better than I knew the mailman. These guys would show up at my office and we'd all groan because it meant I was being hit with another lawsuit.

And just so you don't get the wrong impression, every one of these suits was thrown out by a judge. The word "frivolous" was used quite a bit.

"Let her be blessed," was my response. "Let her receive our love and our blessing. Forgive her. Love her."

Of course, something way deep inside me was saying, "Let me go beat the shit out of her!" But I was keeping that negative voice locked away in solitary confinement. That voice was not going to drown out my other, finer voices. If I was going to be godlike, damn it, then I was going to conduct myself on a high, all-knowing, all-forgiving level. I was going to be God herself, if that's what it took.

"Send her love," I'd tell the girls who worked for me. "Send her joy." Where in reality what we should have been sending her was lithium. Prozac. Arsenic.

It should come as no surprise that life at this heavenly level was more than I could comfortably sustain. There's only one person I've ever known who came close to existing honestly on that high plane. My ex-stepmother-in-law. My ex-husband's father's second wife.

She was the most spiritual person I've ever known, though she never read a book on the subject or talked about it or did anything overtly "spiritual." But she was at total peace with life and the world and everyone in it. She was serene and tranquil and sweet-tempered. She was so spiritual that she never had to devote a moment's thought to the subject of spirituality. It would be like a bird thinking about flight. She seemed to understand all human behavior, no matter how low or mean, and because she understood all, she forgave all, and because she forgave all, she went about her life unburdened by the kind of angry, bitchy moods that make the rest of us such a pleasure to be around.

I would try to rile her up. I'd say to her, "Shirley, nobody can be this good."

"I'm not so good," she'd say. She was so good she was embarrassed. Somewhere along the way she just decided that she was going to face the world with love, and she wasn't going to pick and choose. To her, everybody was wonderful, and even if they weren't, they were.

But even she had one person she couldn't forgive, one person she really and truly hated without apology. Hitler. Him she hated, and since she was a Holocaust survivor you can give her that one, I guess. The Nazis wiped out her entire family, parents and siblings. But that was all she needed—one person to hate. Whereas the rest of us can't make do without a dozen or so.

Even I, a paragon of spirituality and acceptance, was unable to remain for long at the lofty perch to which I aspired. For me, sending love to every son of a bitch who gave me misery was too much work. It was phony.

So when my son died and the former friend who had been suing me left and right showed up at the funeral, I ordered my sister Judy, "Get her the fuck out of here!" It was maybe the only coherent thought I had that entire day, but it was a good one.

Today I have settled into a place I can occupy without getting a nosebleed. I am no longer a celestial bearer of wondrous love. But I'm not a miserable witch either.

I walked by a fancy ladies' clothing store on a tony stretch of Madison Avenue and saw in the window a sweater I liked. I was dressed casually that day, having had no intention of shopping, but I ran into the store.

"I'd like to see the sweater in the window," I told the clerk.

"It's very expensive," she replied.

"I can imagine," I said. "May I see it, please?"

"It is *extremely* expensive," she said, this time a little more firmly.

It suddenly hit me that this jackass thought that I had somehow stumbled into her little jewel box of a shop thinking I was in Kmart. And she believed that if she treated me like trash I'd slink away. Boy was she wrong.

"Oh, I am sure of that," I said. This time I gave her my biggest smile. To look at me you'd think I was getting the most courteous treatment ever. "Now—show it to me." And I stood still. Smiling.

Suddenly, she was the one who was feeling off guard and uneasy. But only because I was clearly having a perfect day.

She got the sweater. I liked it. She found my size. I bought it. Look, I don't spend that kind of money (*what kind? don't ask*) on a sweater every day, but once in a while I'm worth it. And the satisfaction of watching that awful snobby bitch squirm brought me almost as much pleasure as the sweater itself.

Here's another example. A friend of mine once owned a shop in Westchester, and her partner was a very wealthy woman. So wealthy that she refused to even acknowledge anyone whose net worth didn't approach her own, and that included me. I'd go into the shop to see my friend and I'd say hello to this idiot, and the woman would just cut me dead. She'd ice me till I shivered.

"I refuse to come to your store," I complained to my friend after a while. "That bitch makes me feel like dirt."

Flash forward to Mike Myers becoming a big success. I'm walking down the street in New York one day and I hear somebody yelling my name from across the street. It's her, my friend's partner.

"What do you want?" I asked her.

"How are you?" she said.

"How am I? I'm the same as I was twenty-five years ago when you wouldn't condescend to speak to me." And with that I walked away.

Then, a few months later, I'm in the studio where *Saturday Night Live* is just about to air. A young man comes up to me, introduces himself, and says he had just gotten hired there.

Then he adds, "I know a really good friend of yours."

"Oh?" I say. "Who's that?"

And he mentions this woman's name.

"Who?" I say.

He repeats it.

"Never heard of her," I said. It just came out.

"Oh, she's in business with your friend," he said.

"I know my friend's partners," I said, "and she's not one of them. You know something? This is the kind of thing that happens to me all the time now, since Mike became famous. The poor woman just must have latched on to this thought. But I've never heard of her."

He stood there dumbfounded.

"You know what?" I said. "If you're really her friend, don't even mention this to her. It would just humiliate her."

Now, how lowdown and mean is that? But at least I recognize it as such. I don't try and rationalize it or make excuses. I am not celestial. I am not at perfect oneness with the universe. Chances are I never will be. I occasionally exhibit a flaw.

For example, from time to time I still call people stupid.

But myself? Never. Never ever.

If that's not progress, I don't know what is.

15 Try It, It Works for Me: The F-Word

I met them in my Canyon Ranch workshop, and they were just about as sad and anxious and close to the breaking point as two people can be. The source of their woe was easy to figure: They had just institutionalized their little boy, who was born profoundly retarded. I'm talking about a kid with needs way beyond what this poor couple could ever hope to manage.

So no wonder they were pretty bad off. Having such a child is a blow. Facing up to the fact that your own baby is more than you can handle is pretty tough too. And then add on the terrible guilt that comes with placing your flesh and blood in an institution.

Now, I know what you're thinking—if they wanted to keep their kid at home and care for him they could have. And maybe you're right. But they knew what they could manage, and I think they knew that had they kept their son at home, maybe they would have crumbled from the stress—which wouldn't have done that kid a bit of good. Look, I have no right to judge them from this safe distance and neither do you, and anyway we're getting off the point.

People come to my workshops looking for answers, and sometimes I can provide them, but sometimes I'm out of my league. What could I or anyone else possibly say or do to two such people to bring them peace? Could I make a dent in that kind of pain? Do I know any magic words?

"What did you two used to do before for fun?" I asked them, pretty much out of the blue. I was groping, I'll admit it.

They exchanged a look.

"We used to go square dancing," he said.

"Aha!" I said. I'm nothing if not eloquent. "When's the last time you went?"

"Before the baby was born," she said.

"Listen," I said, "would you mind showing us a few of your steps?" Now, this wasn't my big Thursday night performance for one hundred-plus in the lecture hall. My workshops usually involve only half a dozen or so people in a small meeting room.

"We need music," he said.

"Oh, let me handle that," I said, and then I—Linda McGoy from O-O-O-O-Oklahoma—began to sing something intended to approximate a country fiddle at a hoedown.

Did they do-si-do? They sure did. Promenade left? You bet. Did they feel like a couple of dopes doing all this in front of strangers while I made noises like a cat with a virus? I guarantee it, but in my workshops everybody has to act like a fool, so it was their turn.

"Please do me a favor," I said when they were through. "When you get back home, go out square dancing again. One night a week, go do. You need a little fun in your lives. Who knows—maybe it'll help." They promised they'd try it.

A few months later this couple returned to the Ranch. They sought me out one day, grinning.

Did my advice send all their pain and anxiety away?

What are you, nuts? That's impossible. That's a fantasy. If you're thinking such a thing could happen you need to go back to page one and start reading all over.

Were they a little better off than they had been? Was their load a little lighter?

Yes. They told me so. Things were better. Not great. Better.

Did square dancing make them forget they had a tragic child? No. Did it erase the worry, the stress, the guilt, the shame? No.

Was it fun? Yes. And is fun better than no fun?

Yes. Fun is better than no fun.

Do you need a book to tell you this?

And yet I know people who spend seventy hours a week at their jobs, ten hours a week commuting to and from those jobs, an hour a day tracking and trading their stocks online, another hour a day on the treadmill, fifty minutes twice a week on the shrink's couch, and maybe forty-five minutes a *month* on fun. When they can spare the time.

Let me ask you something. Doesn't fun feel better than money? Better than six-pack abs? Better than anything your psychiatrist has told you in the last hundred or so sessions? So why do you shortchange yourself on fun?

Fun is good for you! You need fun! See that couple with the child in the institution? They needed fun! It didn't make a bit of difference in their problems. But overall, it made their lives a little better. Before, they just had misery. Now they have misery *and* fun. Isn't that better? That's exactly what life is all about—misery and fun. You're going to get the first part whether you want it or not. So you had better make sure you get the second part too.

I love the expression that some people throw around when they decide that a solution being offered just won't cut it:

"That's like putting a Band-Aid on cancer," they'll say.

I have a question. Does the Band-Aid make the cancer hurt a little less? I'm not asking if it cures the cancer. Only if wearing the Band-Aid, for whatever insane, illogical reason, makes you feel a little better. Because if it does, then putting a Band-Aid on the cancer is a pretty smart move. Better a Band-Aid than nothing—which is exactly what those snotty gloom-and-doomers are offering you.

A Band-Aid isn't enough? Fine, bring me something better. But if you can't, then shut up and gimme my goddamn Band-Aid. In fact, give me the whole box.

I get excited by the subject of fun.

I'm visiting my daughter and son-in-law.

"Mom," she tells me, "tonight we're going to So-and-so's house for Fun Night."

I promised my daughter I wouldn't name-drop. Not even initial-drop.

"What's Fun Night?" I asked.

"Don't worry, you'll see," she said.

"What do I wear?" I asked, suddenly filled with anxiety.

"It's very casual," she said, casually.

Which is the worst thing she could have said. If she had said, "Mom, it's formal," I'd know exactly what to wear. If she said, "It's dressy," or "It's dinner party," or "It's business," or "We're meeting the Queen," I'd be okay. But casual! What does casual mean anywhere, let alone in Hollywood at the home of her-whose-name-I-shall-not-mention?

So I run out to the mall and spend two hours getting into and out of what I hope are casual clothes and I spend a lot of money and hurry back home to get dressed. In my room I hang each outfit up on a hanger and begin the long, tortured process of figuring out what I'll wear.

So we go to the house, ring the bell, walk in, and are immediately issued T-shirts with our names printed on them. Long T-shirts. Long enough to cover the outfit I had sweated over for the better part of the day.

Into the living room we all pile, where the first game of the night had already begun. It was one of those games where you have to go up to a big easel in front of everybody and draw something and nobody knows what it is but they have to guess. I may be leaving out a rule or two but you know the kind of game I mean.

"*I'm not doing this!*" I hiss to Robin.

"What are you talking about?" she says.

"*I can't draw for shit!*"

"Mom, who cares if you can draw?"

"*Well, I'm not going to make a fool of myself!*"

And of course, at that moment it is my turn. Red-faced, I go to the front of the room, grab a marker, make some feeble attempt at drawing—I was so anxious that today I can't even remember what I was supposed to draw—and return swiftly to my seat. Once there I glance up at the easel. It looks like someone who recently sustained a serious head injury scrawled something on the sketchpad.

Then the next player takes her turn. Her drawing is as feeble as mine. Maybe worse. I instantly feel better and get into the spirit of the evening.

The point here is this: You have to make time for fun. These were all high-powered women in that room. They all had enormous demands on their time and attention. But they all made time for fun. You know who's my favorite tycoon today? Richard Branson. The guy built an empire around Virgin Atlantic Airlines, but you always see him on the news riding his hot-air balloon and flying here and there and having great adventures. I've never seen a photo of him where he wasn't smiling.

You know who used to be my favorite tycoon? Malcolm Forbes. Again, the guy built a business empire and made piles and piles of money. Still, he was riding his motorcycle around and hosting these huge parties and hanging around with Liz Taylor—clearly, the guy knew how to have fun. So if Richard Branson and Malcolm Forbes can find time in their schedules for fun, you and I have no excuse.

Look, you make time to pay your bills. You make time to do your taxes. To floss your teeth. To get a physical. To call your insurance agent. To take your car in for a tune-up and oil change. You make time for every tiresome, nasty, unpleasant, invasive, exhausting, depressing little responsibility in your life. You do it because it's the adult thing to do. The prudent thing. The smart thing.

Well, fun is the smart thing too. You need fun like you need food and water and sleep—to keep you functioning and healthy. Did you eat today? Did you sleep last night? Make time for fun.

You know what's fun for me? Cop shows. Lawyer shows. Detective shows. Going back to my childhood, when I loved Charlie Chan movies. Now I still watch *Columbo* reruns. *Cagney and Lacey. Law and Order.* When I started giving my weekly lecture at Canyon Ranch, it was scheduled for Wednesdays. The same night as *Law and Order.* I couldn't go to the owners and say, "Hey, thanks a million for giving me this opportunity, but could you switch me to another night because the lecture is interfering with my TV schedule?"

No—instead I said, "You know, I think Wednesday is a

little too early in the week for my lecture because all the people who check in Monday or Tuesday don't find out about it in time, so the better night, in my opinion, would be Thursday." That I could say, and I did, and they moved me. But it was only so I could sit in front of the TV and enjoy my secret passion. (You're right, I could tape it, but then I'd have to learn to use my VCR, and I'd rather move heaven and earth than learn to use my VCR. Less complicated.)

Comedy I watch when I feel lousy, but cops and robbers and DAs I watch for love. For fun.

I can't believe I have to convince people to have fun, but I do, every week, at my lectures and my workshop. I ask for a show of hands of all those who make sure to have fun at least once a week. And I probably see three or four hands a month. A couple card players. Some tennis lovers. A dancer or two.

Not long ago an executive of the Ranch attended my weekly workshop for the first time. This particular guy is, well . . . let's be kind and say he's uptight.

He's sitting in this fairly small group of people who are trying to have a good experience and break down some of the walls between strangers. And he's in his chair, ramrod straight, with his arms crossed tightly over his chest. He looked like he was afraid somebody was going to mug him.

While I had everybody else in the room up and dancing, I went over to this man and said to him in a voice no one else could hear, "You have two choices—you can start having fun or you can leave the room at once. Actually, you have a third choice—you can fire me. But I'm not going to allow you to sit here like that another minute."

Son of a gun if he didn't crack a smile. He was up and dancing a second later. The poor guy needed somebody to force him to enjoy himself, but once I did just that he

167

played like a ten-year-old. For weeks afterward he went around the Ranch almost bragging about what I had threatened him with and how he had responded.

Of course, a month later he had gone back to his old self and I haven't seen him smile since. But for that month he had some fun. And it made his life better, I am convinced.

Overwhelmingly, people figure they'll have their fun when they can fit it in. Which for most of them means they'll do without it on a regular basis. It amazes me how people can so easily deny themselves something that makes them feel so good.

There's one thing you hear from almost everyone who has ever tried suicide or given it serious consideration: They are in a lot of pain and it seems as though it will never let up. It's not just the pain of this moment or this day that drives them to suicide. It's the despair they feel—the certainty that the pain will never leave them. That the future will hold no relief.

That's what fun is—relief from the pain or boredom of everyday life. If you can have just a little fun today, it's a sign that maybe the future will hold even more fun for you. Fun isn't just fun—it's hope.

Help Yourself (or Don't)

I don't know if you can tell, but amid all the stories and the shtick this is allegedly a self-help book. In other words, I'll do my part but then the rest is up to you. That's why they call it *self*. You'll read my timeless wisdom and sage advice, but then you'll do whatever you want. You'll listen or you won't. You'll retain it or it'll zoom right out of your head. Chances are I'll never know—I assume you'll make the most of it, but it's out of my hands, and to tell you the truth that's a blessing. How many people can I worry about?

In my real life, I tend to want to do everything for the people I love. If you've got a problem I make it mine, whether you want me to or not. I'm like a field general when somebody I know is in a jam—I'm marshaling forces, I'm barking orders, I'm calling in airstrikes, whatever it takes. If there's one thing I'm experienced at, it's dealing with the garbage life throws at you.

At dawn the phone rings. It's someone I know.

"Are you watching CNN?" she asks.

Now, for future reference, let me tell you that no good news ever started with the words "Are you watching CNN?" If you're watching CNN at dawn I guarantee it's because there's been a bombing or a mudslide or a plane crash or World War III has been declared. CNN at dawn is not a reliable source of happy tidings.

"No, I'm sleeping," I mumble. Of course, by now I'm wide awake, terrified by what I'm about to learn.

Earthquake. Southern California. A bad one too. Highways are collapsing, including the freeway that's maybe two miles from where Robin and Mike live. Maybe there will be even more shocks before it's over.

Boom, I'm ready for action. I start calling them, but of course all circuits are down. Just then the phone rings— it's Robin and Mike, on their cell phone, alive, unhurt, but in the middle of a hell of a mess.

"Okay!" I yell. "Get out of the house now! Get into the car! Head for the airport!"

"Where are we going?" my daughter asks.

"I don't know yet!" I reply. "Take the phone. Once I have you booked onto a flight, I'll call and let you know."

And they're off! Now I spring into action and create a team of assistants. A few minutes later I have four people calling every airline that flies out of Los Angeles, trying to find the next thing taking off. Where, I don't care. Once we begin to narrow it down, I call Robin again.

"How's it going?" I ask.

"Fine," she says. "We're close to the airport! Where are we going?"

"I'm working on it! Maybe Detroit! Maybe Buffalo! Just drive!"

Just then one of my top lieutenants breaks in on the call.

"Toronto!" my sister Judy barks. "Air Canada!"

"Terrific!" I say. "Mike has family there! Gimme the reservation number!"

I get back on the line with Robin.

"Toronto!" I yell. "Air Canada!"

"Okay!" she says. "But Mom—we're in sweatpants and T-shirts!"

"No problem!" I say. "I'll call Mike's brother and tell him to meet you at the airport with winter clothes."

Boom, I'm on the phone to Toronto. I fill Mike's brother in.

"Get them jackets!" I say.

"You got it," he says, and hangs up so he can go shop. Phone rings a minute later.

"Linda!" It's Mike's brother again.

"What?!"

"What color?"

"Uh . . . let me think . . ."

And suddenly it hits me—who the hell cares what color? Jacket color is not part of emergency response. In fact, the emergency—if one existed—is at this point pretty much over. The kids survived the quake without a scratch. They're on their way to Toronto. Meanwhile, I'm still in my pajamas, in a frenzy. I'm still struggling and battling and calling and plotting. I'm fighting my way onto the beach at Normandy. I didn't notice the war was over.

It's a human tendency. Maybe you have it too. Once you get a good grip on a real catastrophe, you almost hate to let it go. I was the commander of the Earthquake Escape Force, and I was doing a pretty good job of it. No shifty tectonic plates were going to get my kids as long as I had anything to do with it.

It was a lesson. Now I pay attention. On those rare occasions when life actually does dish up an emergency, I do my part and then get out of the way. Everybody's better off, me especially.

The phone rings. One of my dearest friends. A lifelong pal. Someone whose welfare is almost as important to me as my own.

A lump. Malignant.

Understandably, she was crazed with fear when she got the news. I was the picture of calm and logic.

"Oh, what do I do?" she said. "What hospital do I go to? Do I need an oncologist? A surgeon? Does the oncologist find me a surgeon?"

"Look," I say, "one step at a time. First thing you need is an operation, right?"

"Right."

"So let's make a list. Number one—find a surgeon. I can help you with that. I know people in the medical field. How many names do you want to choose from?"

"Five," she said.

"Okay, we'll find the top five surgeons for this operation. Then we'll have to make sure whoever you choose is in your health insurance plan. And you need somebody who works in a hospital near you."

So I called another friend whose husband is in the medical field. She did a little research and gave me five top-shelf names. I gave my friend the list with phone numbers attached.

"It's like shopping for anything else," I told her. "You need milk, you go to dairy. You have to focus on one item at a time." And in this way I brought order to her confused mind. She was trying to think of fifty things at once. You can't do that, I advised her. Think of fifty things one at a time. That you can do.

So she did. Came through surgery with flying colors.

After one day in the hospital they want to move another

patient into her room. That's what semiprivate means—no privacy at all.

"You're getting a private room," I told her.

"My insurance doesn't cover it," she replied.

"I don't care. How can you get better in a room with a sick stranger five feet away? I'll take care of it."

And down I zoomed to the financial office, where I turned over my Visa card to cover the difference. Then back up to the floor I zoomed, where I asked to see the private rooms they had available. The one they showed me smelled funny. It smelled sick.

"Can you get somebody in here to clean this room so it smells better?" I asked the nurse.

"We'll try," she said. I knew exactly what was going through her mind: *This broad thinks she's checking into the Four Seasons. Next thing she's gonna ask is where's the concierge.*

Did I care? My friend was trying to beat cancer. She deserved a little extra consideration. And she recovered like a champ, I might add.

Come stay with me a while and recuperate, I offered. The desert's good for that.

So she's out here where everybody's healthy. Walking miles and miles every day. No stresses. No responsibilities. All day in and out of the canyons, looking at cactus, smiling at lizards, thinking serene thoughts. Every day another tremendous, life-changing insight. She's all of a sudden figuring out everything she was doing wrong and how she's going to do it all better once she's back home.

The single major cause of stress and anxiety in her life was money. Now, everybody worries about money, but this woman had genuine cause for deep concern. She and her husband owed the IRS a ton. And they had no realistic hope of being able to pay it off in a timely fashion, which is what the government usually likes.

"Listen," I said to her. "I want to have a serious conversation with you about what you owe them."

"Okay," she said.

"In fact," I said, "I want to give you a couple of thousand, just to get them off your back."

"What?" she said.

"This is not a loan," I said. "Because then you'd just be moving the debt from one place to another. I'm going to give you money. You're going to pay it to the government. And then you and your husband are going to keep up with your taxes so this doesn't happen again. All right?"

"All right," she said.

I was in a position to make that gift. But I didn't feel particularly generous when I did it. My main motivation was selfish—as I said, this woman's well-being was almost as important to me as my own. When she suffers it actually has a negative effect on me. When she's sick I get sympathy illnesses. If anything happened to her I would never totally recover. We're that close. So I was looking out for me when I helped her.

She's with me in Tucson, recovering, and we have a serious conversation about her money woes. Now, this is a woman who has always liked to live high on the hog. She and her husband never quite learned to live on what they made, which is how they got into such a fix. Part of their extravagance was the apartment in New York where they lived. A terrace. A view of the river. On the Upper East Side. Big bucks.

"You've got to move," I advised her.

"I know," she said.

"I realize you love that apartment, but it is literally killing you. The rent is more than you can afford. You've got to move."

"You're right," she said. "I've got to change a lot of

things in my life. We can't go on spending the way we've done. For years the stress has been grinding away at us, killing us. And we've got to stop it now before it's too late!"

Doesn't it feel great when you can help someone you love come to an important realization? Isn't it a terrific feeling to know that you've been part of a moment that changes the course of someone's life for the better?

I have no idea.

"So," I said to her on the phone once she returned to New York, "how's the apartment-hunting going?"

"Oh, I don't know," she said.

"What do you mean?"

"I just love this place."

"I know, but it's making you sick."

"It really isn't."

"It really is."

"It really isn't."

"Why not look in Queens, or New Jersey?" I said. "You'll find a huge place that you can afford."

"Uh-uh," she said. "Too gray."

"Too gray?" I said. "Manhattan isn't gray and Queens is gray?"

"I just *can't*."

"For your own sake, you *have* to."

"I *can't*."

We went on that way for awhile. You can imagine where it ended, just as you can guess where she's living even today.

So who was the dope in all that? Well, I can tell you that my friend exercised less than brilliant logic where her biggest problem was concerned, and that she's still suffering as a result.

But I can also look at my own behavior there and say that I wasn't doing either one of us any favors. You've got to offer advice only sparingly. And when you do, it's got to be in the proper spirit. In other words, you offer and they either take it or they don't. You did your part and that's where your involvement ends. It's like any other gift—once you give it it no longer belongs to you, and so you get no say in how it is used (or not used, as the case may be).

I care about my friend deeply. I care about her so much all I wanted to do was beat the crap out of her and make her see the sensible path. But you can't do that. Either people see it or they don't, and you have to learn to let go so they can make their mistakes just like you make yours.

Can I imagine how I'd react if somebody tried to force me to take their advice? I'd yell in a second.

The lesson here is that when somebody you care about is in trouble, you've got to be very careful not to get too sucked in. It's natural to want to take on somebody else's problem. That's what we call sharing the load. Two heads are better than one. He ain't heavy, he's my brother.

At the same time, you can go overboard. Even good advice can be a burden if somebody is pressuring you to take it whether you want to or not.

The fact is that when somebody you love is in trouble, you've got to tell yourself: Back up a little bit. Resist the natural impulse to pull that person closer to you. Don't try to feel their pain.

This comes into play in my life quite a bit. You know, we who have lost a child are like members of a club we never wanted to join. We all have a lot in common. We connect at a fundamental level, even if we've never met before. And we share something that nonmembers, no matter how close to us, can never be a part of. I believe that the things I've learned about how to cope with the death of a child can be useful to many other people. But I realize that those who have also lost a child will listen most attentively. We hear one another loud and clear. And, I have to be honest, these are the people I want to help most. These people are like my special mission.

But the first thing I tell them always sounds a little hard-hearted.

"Remember this," I tell the parents. "You didn't die. Your child died. You may *wish* you had died instead. But you didn't. It's a nice thought and a typical parental impulse. But life doesn't work that way. So you have to accept that your child has gone down a path alone, and you remain behind. Your life is not over, though you may think it is and wish it were."

I keep going.

"Look," I say, "things would be a lot easier if you *had* been the one to die. There's nothing like dying to put all your problems in perspective. Once you're gone, it's amazing how the normal worries of everyday life seem to just disappear. There were many moments after my son died that the pain seemed unbearable. At those times, death would have felt like hitting the Lotto. And still, I didn't die. I didn't kill myself, though that's a decision I could have made. Dying would have been easier than living and yet I chose life. We all have thus far chosen life. And so, having decided to live, now what?"

I don't think of it as tough love or any of that nonsense. But you've got to create some emotional distance between you and the person you're trying to help, and you've got to do it at the moment when he or she needs you most. If that's not one of *the* most annoying facts of life, I'd like to know what is.

17 Try It, It Works for Me: The Good News

Y ou don't eat poison, do you?

Not unless you're trying to do yourself some serious harm, I mean. You probably don't drink industrial toxins either, or nuclear waste. Or if you did, you'd at least realize that you were up to no good. People today can't go to McDonald's without feeling guilty about the junk they're putting into their systems. Those of us who eat crap or drink booze or smoke accept the fact that we're hurting ourselves. We know there will be a price to pay.

That knowledge doesn't always stop us from doing it. But we know what we're doing.

And yet we consume all kinds of foulness without even noticing. We expose ourselves to the most powerful infections and pollutants in existence. We willingly digest sadness, pain, degradation, violence, meanness, chaos, mayhem, despair, hate, catastrophe, calamity, and worse, on a daily basis, and refuse to believe we're doing ourselves a bit of harm.

Crazy, right?

I'm not a neurologist or a psychiatrist, but I know this much: Inundating your mind with negativity is no good for you. Battering your mentality with hopelessness and fear and rage isn't doing yourself any favors. It doesn't do anything positive for your moods. It's not the kind of experience that sends you skipping down the lane with a song of love in your heart.

People have to learn to treat their minds at least as well as they treat their stomachs. You have to feed your head the right stuff.

You can't let the news media decide what goes into your head. They call it "the news" but in truth it's "the bad news," because when do you ever see or read about something when it goes right? Ninety-eight percent of what's on local TV news is bad news—murder, arson, robbery, insanity on the loose. Even the weather—every tornado and hurricane, no matter where it is, makes the eleven o'clock news, but when's the last time you saw extensive coverage of a sunny day? Network news is only slightly better—maybe ninety-five percent bad news. There, famine and war and hate are the big stories of the day. How many reporters and camera crews are assigned to cover love? When's the last time they broke in on regular programming to bring us a live broadcast showing people of different races getting along?

Newspapers aren't much better. True, you can find the movie listings and recipes every Wednesday, but what's on page one? If you start reading there, by the time you reach the food section you'll be too depressed to eat.

Even a hard-bitten realist has to concede that the good things in life outweigh and outnumber the bad by a mile. But if your view of the world is influenced by what you read or watch on TV, it's easy to forget that fact.

This is not to suggest that I go around in total ignorance. I watch CNN like everybody else, but I make good use of the remote control. I want to know when there's trouble in Kosovo, but when the media decides to show ultra-graphic photos, I click away. Information is one thing. Shoving my nose in the blood and the tears is something else. I have enough emotional cushioning to live with the information. But TV has the power to make us all eye-witnesses, and I can't function at my best if I'm forced to take a front-row seat to all global suffering.

And neither can you, I don't care who you are.

Years ago, nobody made much connection between the food they ate or the air they breathed and their sense of well-being. People pretty much ate and drank and smoked what they wanted without giving too much thought to the effect on their bodies. Only "health nuts" insisted on clean air and water and lots of fruits and vegetables and vita-mins and minerals.

Today, we all accept that close connection between what we eat and how we feel. We're all health nuts, and our lives are longer and better as a result. Still, we persist in thinking that we can take any nasty junk into our heads without suffering the slightest ill effect from it. Someday soon, that notion too will seem hopelessly outdated, old-fashioned, and ill-informed.

Most of the TV watching I do is with my VCR. That's the best way there is of controlling what's on. Right now I've got Mel Brooks up in my bedroom. One night a few years ago I was flipping through the channels when I hit *Mad About You,* the sitcom, on a night when Mel Brooks was a guest star. I was on the verge of throwing up that night—I laughed so hard that night that I was actually retching and heaving. I mean, that's funny, right? Turns out he appeared on three shows, so I got all of them on tape. I watch those shows now and I feel physically dif-

ferent afterward—it's like a workout. I can't help smiling
when they're over. Every day I spend maybe thirty minutes watching those shows. I fast-forward around, to save
time, skipping right to Mel. You can keep all your hunks—
if I were on a desert isle, Mel Brooks is the man I'd want
with me. He changes my day.

Another big VCR hit in my room is Roberto Benigni's
acceptance speeches when he won his Oscars. Whenever I
catch myself slipping into a low mood, I sit in front of the
TV and play the tape over and over until I find myself
catching a little of his joy. Only when I feel better do I
turn Roberto off. It's done wonders for my Italian too.

Norman Cousins proved all this brilliantly years ago, but
it's worth repeating—laughter causes physiological changes
in human beings. I tell everyone at my workshops to stock
up on funny movies or comedy tapes by whoever it is that
does it for them, whether it's Jack Benny or Martin Short
or *"I Love Lucy"* (or Mike Myers, for those of true taste).

I have a whole arsenal of musical instruments in my
home, most of them the kinds of percussion things that
kids love to bang. I'm a very accomplished triangle virtu-
oso. Spend fifteen minutes playing loud, noisy instruments
badly and it cheers you up. Music is a great way to stop
yourself from moping. Turn on the stereo and sing along,
and you automatically turn away from bad thoughts. No
matter how bad your voice is, this works. In fact, sometimes the worse your voice is, the faster it will cheer you
up. (And if not you, it'll probably make other people laugh.)
At my workshops, everybody has to sing. No matter how
humiliated they feel to start, before their song is over they're
laughing.

In the music department, nothing lifts my mood like
Streisand, no surprise there. My son-in-law didn't have to
exaggerate my devotion to her. I have everything she's ever

recorded, and I listen to it at home and in the car. I sing along too, poor Barbra—she'll never know what kind of off-key duets she takes part in. I'm crazy about show music too, Sondheim especially, but almost any kind will do. Mandy Patinkin. Ethel Merman! I cannot listen to her without feeling on top of the world. I don't let the radio stations decide what music I'll hear and when I'll hear it. Music is too powerful an influence to leave it to strangers to decide.

I program the soundtrack of my life.

There's a point to all this: Laugh, sing, dance, or do anything to get you outside yourself. The pain and suffering are inside, and there you are too, trapped with them. The minute you get outside yourself, you begin to escape the sadness. That's when you're on the road back. Once you can do that, you realize you can manage yourself. You're not a captive to the sadness inside. If you can shoo away the negative and hang on to the positive for five minutes today, maybe you'll do it for half an hour next month. If a funny movie makes you laugh a little now, you'll laugh a lot someday.

The kind of control you must maintain over your outside influences can't be limited just to TV, papers, and music either. In my living room, for instance, I have lots of family photographs. Pictures of my sister and me when we were children. Smiling. My daughter's wedding photo. A very happy day. A photo of me with my father, a man whom I love though I have no recollection of him, ever. I have pictures of Jordan up there too. In my favorite one, he put pretzels over his eyes, like glasses. Some days I'll look at those pictures and just smile. Other days I burst into tears and weep and weep. It's completely unpredictable. I never know how I'll react.

In every photo in my living room, people are smiling.

I won't put up any other kind. My Aunt Pat, my mother's sister, was the closest thing I had to a real, loving mother. But I have no pictures of her with a smile. So she's not in my living room.

My mother—there are no pictures of her smiling. And she was not a happy influence in my life, that's for sure. So there's not a picture of my mother in the entire house. This is how I've edited the snapshots that I see every day: If you're not smiling, you're not here.

I even extend this kind of control to the people in my life. I don't care who it is or how much I love them—if they depress me, I don't see them. Some people don't even mean to be depressing. They can't help it. Everything that comes out of their mouths is defeat and despair and disappointment. Hang around with somebody like that and you'll end up infected too. Their sadness is like a virus. One of my best friends even fits that description—and I no longer have anything to do with her. I miss her friendship, but being near her actually did me more harm than being without her. So I did the tough thing and cut off the relationship. It sounds hard-hearted, I know. But consider the alternative—I'll be a nice friend, a nice, terminally depressed friend. Who needs that?

I have a relative I call My Luck, because every story she tells me either starts or ends with the words "My luck!" Everything bad happens to this woman. She can't escape unhappiness for even a second, if you believe her version of events. She's never spent an hour with a therapist or anyone else who might help her. She's never devoted fifteen minutes to thinking about why it is she feels like she lives inside an endless thunderstorm.

Even though we're related, I have to say this: Who needs her?

Not me. So I stay away. I don't call. I don't write. And

when I see she's online the same time I am, I turn off my computer.

She knows it too, and she tells the family all about it.

"Linda's lost her mind!" she says. "She's not like she used to be!"

Well, she's wrong on the first count but right on the second. To me, talking to somebody who depresses you is crazy, I don't care who they are. Nobody needs family members like they need air and water. She's absolutely right that I'm not like I used to be. Because I used to be the kind of person who would put up with my cousin regardless of how bad she made me feel. I'd listen to her go on and on about how lousy her life is and how lousy my life is and how lousy life itself is, and I'd wish the whole time that she'd shut the hell up, but I'd never even interrupt her.

So I lump this relative in with violent movies and depressing news programs—not for me.

On the other hand, my cousin Barbara and I see completely eye to eye on everything. We made an actual pact with each other—we'd never judge each other's actions negatively. And we'd complain once in a while, but never for too long. Oh, we can be vicious when judging other people. But to her I can do no wrong, and vice versa. We may not really always think that way, but we'll never say a discouraging word. It's one reason I love her so much.

Once in a great while she'll say something like this:

"Linda, I'm really upset with you, because the last time we talked you said this and that and later when I thought about it, I was mad."

"Okay," I'll say back, "I'm gonna take responsibility for that. You are right. But now I want you to tell me what's going on in your life that made you take such offense at what I said. Because if I had said that under normal conditions you wouldn't have been upset in the slightest."

I mean, that's love. That's closeness. We can criticize each other once in a while as long as we do it gently. We can even sound gloomy as long as we do it right.

I can always tell when she's feeling really low. I'll say:

"Barbara, how are you?"

"Fabulous," she'll reply.

Which means: Really shitty.

"Well, I am so happy to hear that," I'll say, which means: I can tell you're feeling low and my heart is with you.

"I'm having just the best day of my life," she'll say, which means: I have never felt so low.

"Great!" I'll say. "Have you had a nap yet?" That's actually a bit of truthfulness, because when she feels blue she sleeps.

"Oh, yeah. I've had one already. I'll definitely have two. I may even try to squeeze three naps in today."

At that point we both crack up. It's our way of dealing with reality without letting it control us too much. It acknowledges the pain, but fights it off by refusing to give an inch. We snub the pain and take a little victory from that. It makes us laugh, which is the main thing. It's a cheap trick, but it's a cheap trick that works.

I recall an interview with Beverly Sills, the opera diva. She has a daughter born deaf, who'll never hear her famous mother's thrilling voice. The interviewer asked Beverly how she copes with this and other sad circumstances, and she replied, "I smile on the outside, hoping the inside gets the message."

One thing I don't have to worry about is reading depressing or otherwise damaging books. That's because I'm still on the reading jag I started back before my son died— books about spirituality, reading that offers me wisdom or consolation or hope. *The Diary of Anne Frank*—I've read it dozens of times, and I gain strength from it every time. I've read hundreds of these books, more than anybody I know. And the good ones I read over and over again. Once in a while I try to read something else—current events, or a novel—but after a page or two I give up. I find that I'm just not engaged by what I read. I'm still a seeker, and I don't want to waste time reading for entertainment when there's still so much wisdom I have left to absorb. Though to be honest, I sometimes wish I could bury myself in a juicy, smutty Jackie Collins novel, just for a break.

MY ALL-TIME FAVORITE COMEDIES

I think laughter is so important that I'm going to list both TV shows and movies.

Funniest Movies:

1. *The Producers*
2. *High Anxiety*
3. *The Jerk*
4. *Blazing Saddles.* Are you beginning to suspect that Mel Brooks makes me laugh?
5. *Annie Hall*
6. *Austin Powers: International Man of Mystery.* My unbiased opinion.
7. *Austin Powers: The Spy Who Shagged Me.* Ditto.
8. *Liar, Liar*
9. *A Day at the Races*
10. *The Bellboy*

Funniest TV Shows:

1. *Mary Tyler Moore Show*
2. *Dick Van Dyke Show*
3. *Rhoda*
4. *"I Love Lucy"*
5. *Seinfeld*
6. *Mad About You*
7. *M*A*S*H*
8. *Everybody Loves Raymond*
9. *Brooklyn Bridge.* Nobody watched it, but I loved it.
10. *Laverne and Shirley*
11. *Taxi.* My all-time favorite.

18 Jews in Cyberspace

I am maybe the world's worst when it comes to technology. Fortunately, I have a friend who's good at it, and she got me a computer and plugged me in and wired me up and found me a place in cyberspace where I belong—a chatroom for Jews over fifty.

It's a great source of enjoyment, and I'll tell you why: If you can't sleep at night, you go to this room, and there're always a few Jews in there. Because Jews over fifty don't sleep. So, thanks to Jewish insomniacs, you never have to be lonely. I have no idea why Jews over fifty no longer sleep through the night. They used to, I'll bet. But they don't any longer. A few hours here. A few more there. But otherwise they're awake and online.

I am a Jew over fifty who normally does sleep. But sometimes I have a leg pain thing going on, which keeps me up and down all night. When that happens, I turn to AOL.

The other night I did this, and sure enough, there were maybe twenty-five Jews in there, wide awake.

"Don't you people ever sleep?" I asked.

"Sure, for four hours," somebody replied.

I live out in the desert, far from my family and old friends, so chatrooms are perfect for me. They're a godsend. I manage to meet people with whom I have lots in common, especially women who are roughly my age and intellectual capacity. There are many people in there at any given time, but you find yourself locking in on a few you really like, and then you seek one another out.

One of my closest friends today is someone I met in the chatroom. She and I hit it off, and then we got to e-mailing each other, and she found out I work at the Ranch, which was where she was headed a few weeks later. I told her to call when she got here, and we met, and we're fast friends now.

People in the chatroom hate her because she's really rich—I mean mansions and yachts and staff rich, not just nickel-and-dime rich—and she's really well-adjusted. She's a happy person, which drives people nuts. You can be rich and miserable, or poor and happy, or even poor and miserable, but rich and happy is too much for other people to bear. If you ever become rich and happy, learn to keep it to yourself.

Lots of people in the chatroom, especially the older ones, are on a fixed income. They hear her say she just got back from Monaco and they want to reach through the wires and strangle her. If they only knew that she's gorgeous too.

"I was hoping you'd be really ugly," I said when we finally met in the flesh.

"I'm sorry to disappoint you," she answered.

I have another new friend I call Martha Stewart. She's a schoolteacher in Northern California, and she is a total domestic goddess. A perfectionist. Does everything herself, by hand, strictly homemade. And she does everything well. She's so homemade that even though we correspond by e-mail, she also sends me letters—long, expressive letters in the most graceful handwriting you can imagine. She makes her own furniture and sends me pictures. Sets the most lavish table imaginable. Every dish an elaborate creation made from scratch.

The other day she e-mailed me that she had been in her backyard, up on a ladder, picking cherries from her tree to put into a pie.

"Let me tell you a story," I wrote back. "I went to my daughter's house in Los Angeles, and in their yard is a whole section of lemon trees. And each tree has tons of lemons. One day I go to the supermarket and bring home a big bag of lemons. My daughter sees it and says, 'Mom, are you nuts, we have a whole backyard full of lemons!'

"I said, 'Yeah, I knew that, but I didn't think you wanted to pick them. I figured they were more or less for decoration—like Christmas trees.'"

My friend cracked up. We couldn't be more different in the household duties department. I even told her my least favorite story about me and cooking.

One year, a long time ago, when I was still married and my kids were small, I decided that I was going to do Thanksgiving dinner. All my life, either my mother did it or my sister Judy did it. Never me. I was always the one who needed a map to find the kitchen. I just never took great pleasure in being the chef, and as a result I never bothered to become any good at it.

This year, for a reason I can no longer recall, I got it into my head that I would show them all that I could do a Thanksgiving dinner as well as anybody else. In fact, I had seen a recipe for stuffing in a magazine, and it sounded so good and tasty that I figured I would make it and knock everybody's socks off.

So comes the big day, and I get out the recipe, and I follow it to the letter, and roast the birdie and summon the family to the table, and . . .

The stuff that goes inside a doll's head? That's what my turkey stuffing resembled. It was beige and dry and tasted like chunky sawdust. You can imagine it was a hit with my loved ones. They still won't let me live it down, to where I actually become annoyed at the mention of it. And they mention it all the time.

But that hasn't prevented me and Martha from becoming great pals.

I have another close online friend, one who lives in Chicago. She's extremely bright and funny, and she suffers from serious depression—I mean devastating—from time to time. We've discussed that fairly honestly, which is why I wasn't totally surprised when one day she e-mailed me that she was going to kill herself.

She was going to take a kitchen knife and slash her wrists open, she had decided. Thank God for AOL instant messaging, so I could respond in a second when I read it.

Now, I have no experience at managing suicide attempts. I leave that to the pros. But when I saw what she wrote, I didn't freak. I immediately took the reins and decided that I was going to help her out of this jam.

"You know," I said, "you're going to make quite a mess."
Silence from her end.

"You're going to end up with your entire floor covered in blood. Not to mention what you'll look like. And don't tell me you'll use pills. Because most of the time, people who try that end up throwing up their guts."

That prompted a glorious "LOL"—computerese for

"Laugh out loud." Meaning that I had gotten her to giggle, at the very least.

Next thing I got her to tell me her shrink's name and phone number. So while we were still instant messaging each other back and forth, I called him and described what was going on. Tell her to call me at once, he said. So I messaged her and told her to telephone him, and I kept e-mailing her while they talked and set up an emergency appointment. My friend and I remained in touch via computer even as she got dressed to leave for the doctor's office. He put her on a pill and it wasn't long before her spirits had lifted and the crisis had passed.

I find it amazing how close I have become to these women, considering that virtually all our contact is online. In e-mail you can't rely on gestures or facial expressions to make your point—you have to really say exactly what you mean. You must truly express your feelings if you're going to be understood. And there are no distractions there either—you can't go shopping together, or see a movie, or do lunch. All you can do is talk, which means you can become truly close in a short amount of time. As I started by saying, I am lousy with technology, but it has done pretty well by me.

In fact, the only times I've gone wrong with my chatroom acquaintances have been times I've tried to turn them into real-world friends.

Not long after I moved to Tucson someone in the chatroom mentioned that she was coming to town for a long vacation. So we agreed to meet when she arrived.

"Why don't we meet at the mall?" she asked.

"Fine," I said. "How about Macy's, in the cosmetics section?"

"Fine," she wrote back.

So I get there, and I wait, and wait, and forty-five min-utes after the appointed hour she arrives.

"My God," I said, "I thought you weren't going to show."

"I'm always late," she replied.

And at that point alarms went off in my head and I thought: What the hell kind of excuse is that? *I'm always late.* She might as well have said: *I'm always rude.*

This was nobody's idea of a sweet little Jewish grand-mom, I thought. This was some tough broad from the 'hood or somewhere. But I figured, look, we're here to meet and have dinner, let's move on.

We choose a restaurant there in the mall and take a table.

"I guess this is beneath you," she said once we sat.

"Why on earth would you say that?" I said. I was really startled.

"Well, you look like a fancy lady."

"Gee," I said, "nobody ever accused me of that before."

"No," she said, "you look like you have money. I saw your car."

"You mean my leased Jeep," I said.

"And your clothes look fancy. Your jewelry too. And you know what? I have to tell you this right now—I hate New York Jews."

I'm practically speechless.

"You're telling me you hate me?" I finally said.

"I'm not telling you that," she answered. "I just don't like New York Jews."

"You know what?" I said. "This is not going how I thought it would. This is not a nice dinner out in my book."

"I said you were a fancy lady," she shot back.

"Okay," I said, "let's just forget this night ever happened. I'm leaving now. Good night."

"Do what you want, fancy lady," she yelled at my back.

Can you beat that? Well, believe it or not, I can!

Another lady I ran into online was also coming to town and wanted to meet. I can't let one bad experience keep me alone in the house forever, right? And this woman was actually funny, which to me is the best thing a person can be. So when she suggests dinner, I'm all for it.

"Let's meet at Red Lobster," she said.

Well, right away I was a little leery. I can't do Red Lobster. Something in me just recoils, and if you want to call me a fancy lady too, that's your prerogative.

But the Red Lobster was near my apartment, and I knew I couldn't get too lost on the way, so I said fine.

"See you at four," she wrote back.

Four? Who eats dinner at four? But I was agreeable. And at least we didn't have any trouble picking each other out, because at four the place was deserted.

She was pleasant enough, and nice enough, which was a good start. Then the waitress came and the lady told her, "We'll have two orders of the cracked crab special."

"Wait a second," I said. "I don't want cracked crab."

"But it's the special," she said. "All you can eat for $12.99."

"I understand," I said, "but I don't want crab, I don't care what it costs."

"But it's a really good deal," she said.

"But it's not what I want," I said.

"But it's the special of the day," she said.

"But I'm not having it," I said.

"Oh, get what you want then!" she said.

And once again I am asking: *What the hell did you get yourself into here? Why do you attract so many insane people?*

"I'll have the lobster tail," I told the waitress, figuring that they're always frozen, no matter where you get them, so what can go wrong? "But please bring us separate checks." Because the lobster was double the cost of the crab, and the cost, I figured, was a big issue with my dinner partner.

With that, I thought I had cleared away any potential problem that might put a cloud over our dinner. Was I wrong.

By the time we were finished she had gone through six orders of cracked crab. She took "all you can eat" as a dare. She had melted butter running down her chin and onto her clothes. Shoveling crab in like a shark. This was my view as I tried to eat my little lobster tail.

"You look very familiar to me," she said through the shellfish.

"Well, we've never met," I said.

"No, I recognize you from TV or something."

Uh-oh, I thought. She could have seen me on *Rosie O'Donnell* the once or twice I was on, or maybe on some little entertainment news clip. The last thing I wanted was for her to make the connection.

"No, I've never been on TV," I said.

"Yes you have."

"No I haven't."

But she knew. I would have been happy when she changed the subject, except for what she changed it to.

"I'm trying to get a divorce," she said.

"Oh, I've been divorced for many years," I replied.

"My husband beats me."

Now, I know the anonymity of online chats creates an immediate intimacy, but why would this woman tell me this in our first meeting?

"Oh, that's awful!" I said. "You ought to get to a shelter until you're able to move away."

Then she told me her son is a heroin addict, and her teenage daughter is pregnant, and she can't move away from the husband because she has five kids living at home. And she makes $7 an hour and has to turn it all over to the husband, and on and on, every minute worse than the one before. At this point, I know she's either lying through her teeth or so in love with her misery that she has to share it with a virtual stranger. All I can think is: Get me outta here!

And you know what? Despite all the worry about how e-mail and the Internet are turning people into antisocial recluses, I have to say that there's something comforting about the distance it allows us. I love being able to connect to people anytime I want just by turning on the computer. But I like being able to control how close they get to me. As I said, I've made real friends online, people I now see in the flesh. And I've also met acquaintances whom I'm happy to see in the chatroom only. I like to be able to choose.

19 Try It, It Works for Me: The Wise Fool

Considering that I lost my father and my son in traffic accidents, does it come as a surprise that I am slightly worried behind the wheel? It's not that I'm a bad driver. It's just that I'm careful and considerate, which automatically makes me a hazard, especially in and around New York City. I'm the driver who always lets other cars in front of me go—which means I'm also the driver all the other drivers want to kill.

I used to spend a lot of time on the Long Island Expressway, where polite drivers go only at great peril. I got so tired of being cursed at and threatened and given the finger by raging residents of Nassau County that one day I went to a novelty shop and bought a pair of those plastic-glasses-eyebrows-nose-mustache things that make even Cindy Crawford look like Groucho Marx. I stuck it in my purse, and next time I did something to offend a fellow driver, and the usual torrent of angry profanity came pouring forth, I put on my mask and stared the other driver right in the face.

Shut him up in a hurry. He even laughed, almost.

See, it's hard to vent serious rage at anyone ridiculous enough to wear one of those stupid masks. It's like—why bother? That woman is clearly too idiotic to understand a thing you're saying.

Ever since I hit on this stunt, I've carried those glasses in my bag. I don't have much call for them in traffic now, among the mellow motorists of the desert. But they still come in handy sometimes.

For instance, sometimes I let my moments of self-pity get out of control, even by my standards. I'll be staring into my mirror, pouring out my heart, my wails and woes. Eventually I realize I've got to snap out of it. Maybe I've got something important to tend to, like my nails appointment.

That's when I get the glasses. I continue telling my sad story to the mirror, only now I do it wearing these stupid glasses. In seconds, the spell has been broken and I'm cracking myself up. It's impossible to take someone seriously when they wear a big nose, fake mustache, and glasses. It's why Groucho Marx wasn't Cary Grant.

In our Canyon Ranch workshops, I always hand these masks out to everyone in attendance. Then I ask the attendees to put them on, face one another, and tell their saddest stories. It doesn't take long before we're all on the floor, howling. If you can laugh while you're in the middle of telling your tale of woe, you must realize that there is hope for you yet, and that you will always be able to find something to smile about. Sometimes that's a pretty important simpleminded lesson.

20 In Search of Your Inner Control Freak

Okay, this is it—the big finish. We've made it to the last chapter, hooray for us all. If I haven't been sufficiently entertaining and instructive thus far, if I haven't lived up to my promises yet, you probably gave up on this book a long time ago. So if you're still with me, thank you from the bottom of my heart, and if not, my sincerest apologies and who the hell asked you anyway?

As a matter of fact, I saved something truly important and maybe even life-changing to pass along to you at this time.

But first, please allow me to tell you maybe the most flattering thing anybody's ever said about me. (Myself excluded, of course.) This comes courtesy of my brother-in-law, Sidney, who's known me since I was a kid. Sidney isn't the kind who throws around undeserved compliments, which makes it all the sweeter.

"If Linda were to walk out her front door one morning and find the entire street flooded," he once said, "she'd just roll up her pants and start walking." In other words, I wouldn't cry and moan and curse the gods and the weatherman and turn around and go back inside and call half a dozen people to find out what I should do.

Now, I realize that as compliments go that's not exactly "Linda has eyes more beautiful than Liz Taylor's." But I'll take it, any day.

The street's flooded? So what? Who cares? What the hell can I do about a flood? Not a thing, except this: I can act as though it isn't there. I can snub it. I certainly can't allow it to slow me down, or change my plans, or even dampen my mood. I wouldn't give that flood the satisfaction. Am I going let a little precipitation control my life? If I do, where do I draw the line? Snow flurries? Drizzle? Dew? Better to just go forth having decided that I won't let *anything* ruin my day. Once you make that decision and learn to stick to it, life suddenly improves a great deal. You no longer waste time waiting fearfully to see if whatever just took place is going to shatter your happiness. You've already decided in advance that it won't—you're going to be happy, damn it, and that's that.

Obviously, I don't mean you're going to go through life brain-dead. You're going to see everything and hear everybody, same as you always have. The obstacles and setbacks and disappointments and heartaches that come everybody else's way will come yours too. As far as I can tell, nobody has learned to control acts of God, fate, or other people, I don't care how many self-help books they've read.

I don't know how apparent it has been, but the one message that keeps popping up throughout this book is this: You've got to get control over how you respond to life. I don't mean you've got to take control of everything all at once. If you can take control of one thing, that's a lot. That's a step.

During my treatment for agoraphobia, I had to learn

how to confront the panic attacks that kept me housebound for so many years. When I felt one coming on, I was taught to tell myself, *Okay, this is a panic attack. It feels awful, but nothing bad is going to happen. You're not gonna die. You're not having a heart attack. It's in your head, not anywhere else. So would you prefer to just focus on how panicky you feel, or would you rather be diverted by something else?*

Well, who wouldn't choose to be diverted by something else at that horrible moment? I couldn't resort to my usual pastime, though—nobody, I don't care how much self-control they have, can read a book during a panic attack. But here's what I *could* do: I could crochet. You can knit at a time like that because your brain goes on autopilot and directs your fingers without a lot of thought. So that's what I did. And as I knitted, I'd force myself to look at the yarn. I'd say, "Gee, I love this shade of pink, and boy, what a pretty scarf this is gonna be once I'm through with it . . ."

Before I discovered knitting, I would feel a panic attack coming on and I would just lie there, filled with dread, waiting for it to smash into me. It would be like looking up in the sky and seeing a piano hurtling downward on you from a high floor—and then not being able to move out of its way. I'd just watch that piano getting bigger and closer every second, until—*wham!*

Miraculously, my brain steered itself off my panic and onto crocheting. It took a lot of work on my part, but that's really how it happened—I trained my mind to stop focusing on the panic. And once you stop focusing on the panic, it loses its hold on you. I grabbed the steering wheel inside my head and veered away from panic and toward . . . *knitting!* But this was truly demonic knitting. This wasn't just a little relaxed clicking of the needles while I watched TV. I was getting one panic attack after another back then. I could have seven a day, no problem. I remember the night

I knitted a sweater—an entire sweater. It's close to impossible for anybody to do that, but I did. I knitted constantly, furiously, all night long. I finally gave in to exhaustion when the sun rose, and I went to sleep. And I had a sweater—a sweater I hated, just because of what it represented in my life. I was happy to give that ugly thing away.

That chapter of my life was an incredible battle for control, believe me. That was one unforgettable lesson in how you can decide your responses to even extraordinary forces.

I haven't gotten panic attacks for many, many years now, but I still find a need to crochet once in a while. I used to be a white-knuckles flier all the way. Now I am the most relaxed person on the plane. I have a bag of wool and needles always packed for when I have to fly. As soon as I'm settled, I'm clacking away. If knitting could turn away those panic attacks I once had, it can conquer any form of useless anxiety. It's like a zen experience for me. Turbulence? Who cares? A little bumpy up there? Not a problem. Back in the agoraphobia days I had to remind myself that the panic attacks were harmless. In midair it finally dawned on me that no matter how much I worry, I can't control the plane. The pilot has his job. The mechanics have theirs. And God sure has a say in what happens at 31,000 feet. Me? Nothing I can do. If anything goes wrong, I'm going down with everybody else. So why worry?

I built up a very successful commercial casting business in New York, and then I decided to turn it over to a young couple who had been working with me. I still have a stake in the company, at least for a little while longer, at which point they'll pay me off and it's all theirs. For now though, we're partners. One day the woman calls me up for our monthly session of going over the income and profit figures. She tells me that she's gone through all the numbers with a new accounting software program.

Now, since I started the business I have depended on a very reliable, very capable outside accountant. This woman looks after all my financial matters, and thank God for that, because if it were in my hands it would be a mess. This woman keeps all my money in tip-top shape.

But my partner in the casting company decides she'll do the bookkeeping herself. Which is why on this particular day she calls to say that not only is there no profit to share with me, but things have not gone so well and I actually owe them around $30,000.

I, upon hearing this, freak out.

"How the hell can I owe *you* money?" I ask, a little frantic. "You're the ones running the business!"

"Well, I know, but I ran all the numbers and then I double-checked it, and it turns out you owe the business $30,000," she says patiently.

It's a good thing my arms can't fit through the phone lines.

At some point in the discussion I realize that she's done whatever she's done on that damn computer and I'll never figure it out long-distance. What I should do is just hang up, go to bed, and tomorrow morning call my accountant and ask her to go through the books and see what's what.

On the other hand, this woman has just told me that I owe $30,000. Am I going to be able to sleep with that big number hanging like a sword over my head?

So I got off the phone. It was 9 P.M. A Herculean session of talking myself down off the ledge ensued. If I really did owe them $30,000, I told myself, there was nothing I could do to change it. If I didn't owe $30,000, then we'd know that in a day. Suddenly it sunk in that I could stay up all night pacing and thinking and worrying about that money, but it wouldn't change anything: I'd either be out $30,000 *and* a night's sleep, or I'd be out $30,000 and at least I'd enjoyed my slumber. Best-case scenario, I'd get a good night's sleep and then I'd learn that I didn't owe a nickel.

Which is exactly what happened. My poor accountant is the one who suffered, having to straighten out the books and explain to my apologetic friend that she'd made an honest number-crunching mistake. But that's why I pay my accountant.

When I moved to Tucson I found a place to live, but it was just barely tolerable. Too small. And it was new construction, meaning it was flimsy, so that when my neighbor sneezed I said, "God bless you," and when her alarm went off, I woke up.

So I found another apartment complex that seemed perfect. Bigger units. Sturdier construction. One minor problem: a long waiting list. I'd have to give it four or five months, the people in the leasing office said.

Now, I could have put my name on the list, gone home, remained miserable, and waited. Normally that would have been my impulse, just like yours. But for some weird reason, I didn't. I kept returning, over and over, to the leasing office. It got to the point where I knew everybody there by first name. I'd be driving to work, see that I was just about to drive past the complex, and then I'd pull in and pay a visit. I'd linger wistfully over by the display showing the floorplan of the two-bedroom model, the one I wanted. I'd chat with the staff. They'd remind me that someone was just about to move into the sole apartment to become vacant in quite some time. Then I'd leave.

What was I doing? I honestly had no idea. It's not as though I was going to charm myself up to the top of the waiting list. I would have tried bribing my way there if I thought it would have worked. Something inside just kept telling me to go back.

Now, you could call this "trying" of a high—no, insane—degree.

But what happened was that on one of my drop-in visits, I learned that a couple had taken possession of their two-bedroom apartment, driven up with their moving van, looked inside the unit, turned around, and left. No reason given, but they decided on moving day not to take the apartment. Guess who got that apartment that same day? Something told me to persist beyond all reason, and lucky for me I listened. No normal person would have. But then no normal person would have gotten the dream apartment that day either. Can I just write it off to dumb luck? I can, but I won't—I take this as indisputable proof that the universe will smile down on you if it sees that you're trying just a little bit harder than most people.

Psychotherapy has been a great lesson in control for me. I've been seeing shrinks on and off (mostly on) for more than forty years now. Therapy has been my path to understanding who I am. It has also taught me a lot about how we gain control over our lives. You relax and tell your experiences and how they made you feel and what that made you do, and with the help of a therapist you turn it all into your "life story." And when you do that, you begin to create a little distance between yourself and what's happened to you. You even get the chance to take a little artistic license with that story—to decide how you will interpret it, whether it will just add up to one miserable saga, or if it will end up as the tale of somebody who experienced sad things and then prevailed.

You shape the story instead of just letting it exist as a long chain of unhappy events. Once you've gained control of the tale, you've also gained some control over the life— how you see your life can actually affect how you live it. You start out letting the life dictate the story, but by the end the story is dictating the life. As I said, this all begins by creating just a little distance, and that distance can be what keeps you sane. Creating that distance is the first act of control. It doesn't mean you suddenly won't feel any pain, or that the same old things won't happen to you. This momentous action takes place entirely inside your head, which is where all meaningful change occurs.

Here's a minor example of what I'm talking about.

As I mentioned before, every time there's any emotional stress in my life, I feel it first in my teeth. I may not even be aware that something's disturbing my peace of mind. Then I get a toothache, and immediately I ask myself, "Okay, Linda, what's up?" And it's not imaginary pain either. It's the real thing.

Whenever that happens, I immediately go to my good friend and great dentist, Saul Pressner. He immediately gets in there and starts looking and fixing and treating. Before you know it I'm pain-free again.

Once I asked Saul what exactly he did to cure those toothaches. Because we're buddies, he couldn't lie.

"Not a thing," he said.

"What does that mean, 'not a thing'?" I asked, a little alarmed.

"I just look, I clean, I fiddle a bit here and there," he said. "But I don't actually *do* anything. There's nothing really wrong with the teeth or the gums, after all."

And he's right—the source of the pain is in my mind. But the thing to remember is that if the pain is there, the cure is there too. Saul doesn't fix my toothaches. I do. I put my belief in his power, but then it's *my* belief that does the job. I had the power to stop the toothache, clearly, because Saul didn't do a thing inside my mouth.

Once you've gotten control inside your head, you've gotten control of life. That's where all the hard battles are fought. That's where the struggle for control and for dignity and sanity and peace and tranquillity have to be waged. Not in the world. Not among the people who are hurting you or failing you or letting you down or screwing you up. If you think your life is going to change by changing other people, you'll never succeed. Focusing on other people just allows you to go on delaying the real battles you face—the ones in your own head.

I said somewhere in these pages that I'm engaged in a more or less constant conversation with myself, checking to see how I feel, examining every corner of my emotions to make sure I'm happy and hopeful, and so on like that. It's work. Believe me, there are more interesting things I could be doing with my brain. But I do it.

I try hardest to control my thinking, but to be honest, I make an effort to control as much of my life as is humanly possible. And if I fail, I try again, even harder. If I keep failing I say to myself, "Well, that's beyond your control." And if that's true, there's no point in my devoting another thought to it, is there? It becomes like that flood—an intrusion, but one I can do nothing about. And if I can't control it, I ignore it.

Does that sound awfully familiar? It's just another way of stating that bedrock of self-help: Grant me the ability to change what I can, and the serenity to accept what I can't, and the wisdom to blah blah blah. The entire world of twelve-step is based on that little prayer. Well, it turns out to be true no matter who you are or what kind of help you need.

I speak as an expert on this topic and this topic alone. More than most people, I think, I have suffered due to an inability to control my own fate. If there's one thing I've learned, it's that I can't depend on destiny to keep a constant smile on my face. I've suffered an event or two that would spoil anybody's Sunday afternoon. Life has never taken seriously its responsibility to be exactly what I want, and you may have found the same is true for you too.

Look at it this way: Any idiot can be happy when things go right.

In my experience, until you learn this lesson, you haven't got a clue.

I learned earlier than most people to fear loss of control. Now, every child struggles with powerlessness. Every kid has to accept that fact of life. But for me it was brought home in a big way when my father died. I didn't even have the power to acknowledge that, or to feel sad about it. That was taken away when my mother decided to lie about what had happened. Because they decided to hide the truth from me, I couldn't even be who I was—a little girl whose daddy had died. My life was all chaos after that, chaos and confusion, because my mother was so ill-equipped to keep our family going in any kind of normal way. So life was beyond anyone's control. Instead of control, I had fear.

Those are the two extremes of human existence, and we swing back and forth between them. At one end, control. At the other, fear. The more control we have over our lives, the less we fear. The less control we have, the more we fear. We're all captives of the same simple equation.

Even as a child, I sensed that I would survive only by trying with all my might to maintain control over who I was and what I would grow up to be. I hated my mother in large part because of this: I feared I would become her. I felt as though if I didn't struggle against her, I would grow up to be just like her. I've said before that when I began therapy, as a young woman, I had just one goal—not to become my mother. She was like a powerful whirlpool, and I had to swim and kick like hell to avoid being dragged under the sea.

Only now do I see what I did, even as a child. I couldn't control who my mother was. I couldn't control the suffocating, negative influence she was in my life. But I could control how I responded to that influence. Everything I ever did to distance myself from her was a move toward emotional health. So the least sane person I've ever known became the only thing that kept me sane. She was the unhappiest person I've ever met, and if I'm happy today it's thanks to her. I turned her into my own personal poster child for misery. By doing that I took control of her and turned her from a negative into a huge positive. As I took control of her, I broke free of her control over me. Control or controlled—that's life, at least as I see it.

I still go through life in a constant struggle with my mother, who is somewhere (deep, I hope) inside me. I have escaped her fate, I feel safe in saying. The unhappiness, the inability to enjoy or express—there's none of that in my life. But for that I have to thank my mother, for if she had been a better person I would not have had to work so hard.

I guess if you're content with who you are and happy with how your life is going, you don't have much reason to struggle. Who would fight a good time? But if you're unhappy with yourself and the state of your existence, you've got to fight to change. If you don't struggle for control, you're doomed to misery. I would call that the easy way out, if you consider such a depressing life easy. For some people, the path of least resistance, the road that requires the smallest effort, is preferable. I feel sorry for those folks, and believe me, I see a lot of them. They love the easy way out more than the possibility that things may improve, I suppose.

We strugglers and strivers are the ones who are in a constant state of becoming. We're our own greatest inventions. I had to invent myself or run the risk that I would grow up to be my mother—a fate far worse than death.

That should have taught me a lesson I'd carry with me for the rest of my life, right? Don't you think you'd come out of that experience determined never again to allow yourself to be controlled? I thought so too.

But then came the agoraphobia. I don't recommend eleven years of it to anybody. But I have to tell you, there's nothing like it for teaching you what you're capable of doing. When I was cured, I learned the hard way about just how much of life you can control. I was a prisoner of fear for eleven years. It's shameful, to feel so powerless. And then, in ten weeks, it went away—the therapy conquered the agoraphobia, but I was left with the bitter knowledge that I had always possessed the strength to beat it. I just didn't know it, or I didn't know how to use it. Even now I sometimes feel the urge to kick myself over that chapter of my life. I just keep thinking the same thought: *Eleven years of captivity, cured in ten weeks of therapy* . . . If only I had gotten help after one year of agoraphobia, or one week of it. The fact that back then nobody even knew what agoraphobia was, let alone how to treat it, is no consolation, believe me.

And then came yet another form of captivity. I remained in a marriage that made me unhappy from day one. I really did know, on my wedding day, that I was making a terrible mistake. But I went ahead with it. Sure enough, it was a match made in hell. And yet I stayed in it for *twenty-nine years!* I had the power to leave it, I just didn't know it. I would sit up night after night, staring out the window into darkness, with a legal pad and pen in front of me. I'd list all the reasons for leaving my husband. Then I'd list all the reasons I couldn't leave. They were mostly about money and security and the kids. But once they were written on the pad, they took on a power of their own. I was defeated by those lists. By dawn, I'd always have lost my resolve to start my life fresh. I was trapped by pieces of paper.

And then, of course, one day I just announced that I was leaving my husband. And then I left him. I still have no idea why that was the day. I just opened my mouth and out came my leave-taking. It even surprised me. Once I did it, once I actually left, I saw that all those lists meant nothing, all those reasons were meaningless. They held me back because I allowed it. I believed that I could not control my life, and that lack of control was my prison.

My final lesson in control, and how to lose it, and then get it back, was the most painful one yet. You receive the blessing of a child not really thinking that the blessing can be taken away. But is there any greater loss of control over your own well-being? Take it from me, there isn't. That's what really plunged me into my journey, my search for meaning in such a tragic thing.

I've seen plenty of people destroyed by such an event. That could have been me too. Maybe it's because I had already had such a weird, suffering existence up until then, but Jordan's death did something else to me—in a way, it became the event that put me securely on the road to salvation.

Jordan's death was without a doubt the worst thing that ever happened to me. But it was also the thing that forced me to examine my life and find a meaning for it. In a way, Jordan's losing his life is what saved mine. If Jordan hadn't died, I wouldn't have gone to the extremes of self-scrutiny I went to. I wouldn't have pushed myself through so many years of looking for a guru, a sign, a meaning.

And without that, I wouldn't have learned that the meaning of life was in *me* and had been there all along.

Once Jordan died, I truly believe, my brain changed a little. I actually became fearless. The prospect of losing money, or a job, or a friend, or of getting sick, had lost its terror. I had already sustained the worst possible loss. Anything else would be easy, relatively speaking.

I'm writing this book to pass along some of what I've learned the hard way. Maybe that's only partly possible. Maybe you have to go through pain and suffering of your own to really and truly gain wisdom. So fine. If this book makes your life only somewhat easier, I'll be satisfied.

But the fact is that just following my advice won't improve your disposition. If that's all there was to it—feel better and you'll feel better—then nobody would be miserable. And there are a lot of unhappy people out there.

It still takes work. *Your* work. I already did mine, and I continue to do it every day.

Did I tell you about my knee? I was in London, in an impossibly fancy hotel room, getting ready to go to the unimaginably elegant dinner before the awesomely glamorous premiere of *Austin Powers: International Man of Mystery,* the feature film starring my son-in-law. I stepped from the shower onto a floor that, unknown to me, was wet and slick. Up I went, and then down, and the instant I landed I knew I had done something devastating to my knee.

Back to New York I flew the next day, hobbling around on not one but two canes. The doctor examined me and performed tests and all the rest, and discovered that I had torn things up pretty badly.

"Can you lift your foot off the floor?" he asked.

I tried with all my might and got it up maybe one one-hundredth of an inch.

"Great!" he said.

"What did I miss?" I asked.

"Well, it moved!" he said. "There's at least *some* mobility!" Which meant that surgery might be unnecessary, he said, as long as I was willing to endure the picnic that is physical therapy. And I shun exercise when I have two good knees.

But I stuck it out, hating every minute. After a month I could walk with just one cane. After another month, no canes. After three months of physical therapy they did some more fancy tests and found that all the damage had healed.

And guess what?

Your soul is no different from your knee.

If you work it, it works.

Epilogue

Well, here we are, about to say good-bye, at least for the time being. I struggled and fretted over how to end this thing. I wanted to find some words that would stick with you, something that would maybe bring you a little peace and hope and wisdom whenever you thought about it. And naturally, the minute you try to come up with something deep and meaningful, your mind goes blank.

At that moment, however, if you're paying attention, life nearly always steps in and provides.

So I'm fishing around for an ending when I have to travel to New York. Every time I'm there I go visit Jordan's grave. It's something I *have* to do, although to be honest it's not a pleasant experience. I don't go to the cemetery for wistful, profound moments of communion with my son's spirit. I go there and cry my guts out. I feel the wound like it all happened yesterday. I'm filled with sadness and dread before I go, and I'm emotionally drained afterward.

Anyway, on this visit I planned to make the cemetery my last stop, since it's only about five minutes from the airport. I had a 10 A.M. flight, so I arranged for the car service to pick me up at 8:30. By nine the car still wasn't there. Now, if I had been in a real hurry I could have just jumped into a cab and gone. But clearly I was feeling ambivalent, so instead I just waited and fumed. The car came at last, I bitched at the driver a little, and I told myself that due to circumstances beyond my control I'd have to skip the graveside visit this time around.

We arrive at the airport and I head straight to check-in—where I learn that instead of being booked on the ten o'clock flight, I'm on the 12:30. Impossible, I say, and ask the clerk to call my friend who works for the airline, and through whom I booked the flight. She picks up the phone, dials, and learns that he's on vacation this week. Fine, I say, and give her another name in the same office. He's out sick. I give her *another* name. Day off.

I'm furious by this point, so I go sit down, hold my head in my hands, and try to figure out what's going on. Finally I say, "Okay, Linda, time to practice what you preach. The cosmos is telling you to go to the cemetery. So go."

Down I go to the taxi line, jump into one, give him directions to the cemetery, and ask him to wait maybe a hundred yards away from Jordan's grave. He drives off, I go to the spot that I see in my imagination every day, and immediately break down—crying, screaming, heaving, hugging the tombstone. I'm a total wreck, as usual. My suffering is so loud that at one point I look up and there's the taxi driver, wordlessly offering me a tissue.

"What a kind thing to do," I say as I take it. He turns and walks back to his car.

Jewish tradition says that when you visit a grave you leave a stone there. I looked around for a good one but couldn't find anything I liked. It had just snowed, and the ground was mostly covered in white. Then I remembered that recently I had loaned a friend my shawl, and when she returned it she also sent a velvet pouch with a beautiful piece of amber inside. I reached in my handbag and found the pouch, and left that gorgeous stone for my son in heaven.

Then I stood, still crying, and looked down.

"You know what, Jordan?" I said aloud. "This isn't funny. I tell people all the time they have to learn to laugh, but honest to God there's nothing funny in people's tragedies." I keep talking along those lines—how ironic that I'm writing a book telling people that humor and joy are possible no matter what happens, and yet when it comes down to it, sad is sad and nobody can tell me different.

I take a step or two away from Jordan's grave and look down, where I read the inscription on the next tombstone: "Milton Eisenberg, beloved husband of Ruth, fat—"

"What the hell is *this?*" I said. *"Fat?"*

And I stooped down to brush away the snow, and saw "father of Frances and Arthur . . ."

At which point I cracked up laughing. I was hysterical, in fact. I stepped back to Jordan's grave and said, "Thanks, honey, I needed that." Then I kissed his gravestone one last time and walked back to the taxi.

10 TOOLS YOU CAN TAKE AWAY WITH YOU

1. If you're depressed or anxious, see a shrink. Talking can be a cure in itself because sometimes it makes you feel better.
2. Express all your feelings, sorrow and joy and everything in between. Repressing them makes you numb.

3. Play.

4. Rent funny movies.

5. Get outside yourself. If you feel lousy and someone invites you to dinner, make yourself go. (Conversely, if you feel great and someone invites you to dinner, stay home if you want!)

6. Laugh every day.

7. Hang around with positive people.

8. Go to comedy clubs without fear—some bad comics will make you laugh harder than good ones.

9. Write your bad feelings down, and do it over and over again until things change.

10. Sing loud.

Acknowledgments

Judy Myers, my sister, my friend, my rock.
I wish everybody could have had you in their lives.
Rest in peace. I love you.

I thank:

Dr. Dan Baker, therapist extraordinaire, who believed in me before I knew there was a me.

My son-in-law, Mike. You have given me the best ride of my entire life—how much fun it's been and how grateful I am to you.

Cousin Babs, the keeper of my secrets, the best friend anyone could hope for.

To Sid, Jody, Bob, Steffie and her family . . . Michelle and Myron . . . you are my family and I'm grateful to you all.

Also, thanks to Amy Baker, Stacy and Dr. Mark Milner, Ellen Eichenblatt, Roe Basile, Pamela Moffat, Steve Bradfield, and Irene (Sunny) Unger.

To my other family members—had you been a little nicer I would have mentioned you too.

Dr. Saul Pressner. Can you imagine acknowledging your dentist? He's the kindest, most compassionate soul that God has ever put on this earth. Saul, for all your kindness, thank you, and the check is in the mail.

Parker, Chelsea, and Blake, how wonderful to hear you call me Grandma, and how much I love you, kiddies.

My friends Sue Kravitz and Sue Haub, thanks for your constant encouragement and friendship. You both have been my blessings. How lucky I have been to meet you.

Richard Pine, my book agent, thanks for getting me such a hotsy-totsy deal. You did good.

Bill Tonelli, for hearing my voice and going through this torturous process with me.

Jackie Meyer, the art director of Warner Books, for air-brushing me and making me look thinner. You are my goddess.

Rick Horgan, my editor. Your belief in this book has been amazing to me. I still don't know what an editor does, but I'll bet you're good at it. And you're so damn cute.

Jody Handley. Your excitement and enthusiasm for this book overwhelm me.

I suppose this is the oddest acknowledgment yet, but from the heart. I want to thank every cast member of *Law and Order* for making their entrances and exits so quietly that I seldom notice they're gone, and yet the show remains one of my real addictions. (I did, however, notice when Benjamin Bratt left.)

There are people I'd like to thank whom I've never met, or the one I met in passing and, oh, what a one that was.

First, Barbra Streisand, for the endless hours and years of happiness and peace your singing and performing have brought me. I can't thank God enough for putting you on this planet at the same time I was here. You've created masterpieces and you are one yourself. One of the great joys in my life was meeting and spending time with you, and you know what? You didn't disappoint.

Next, Oprah Winfrey, for giving us television at its finest. Oprah, you took the high road and made us all climb the mountain with you. Bless you.

Mel Brooks, for being either very silly or just plain crazy, it doesn't matter. You've made me laugh for so many years now. When I hear "Ladies and gentlemen, Mel Brooks!" I'm ready.

Dr. Wayne Dyer, for your simple words and great wisdom. Without knowing you, I know your heart.

Deepak Chopra, for bringing your brilliance, wisdom, and knowledge to all of us.

And Steven Spielberg: Thank you, thank you, thank you.

And last, but surely not least, to Rosie O'Donnell . . . the child of my heart. Nobody can come close to her goodness, kindness, and caring. Her concern for the kids of the world is astounding. She has brought so much joy and happiness to so many millions of people and asks for so little in return. She just wants you to care about others. She is truly one of God's angels. Rosie, it's an honor to call you my friend.

All the writers in the world: Thank you for sharing your words. What an exquisite escape from the pains of the world. Someone once asked me, what is harder—like I would know—acting, writing, or composing music? My answer to that is, anything that makes the heart soar—and words make *my* heart soar.

I would also thank these people for enriching my life and for always making me laugh . . . Tammy Abraham, Bill Goulding, Shannon Hardin, Eileen and Ned Steinberg, and Barbara and Howard Goldenfarb.